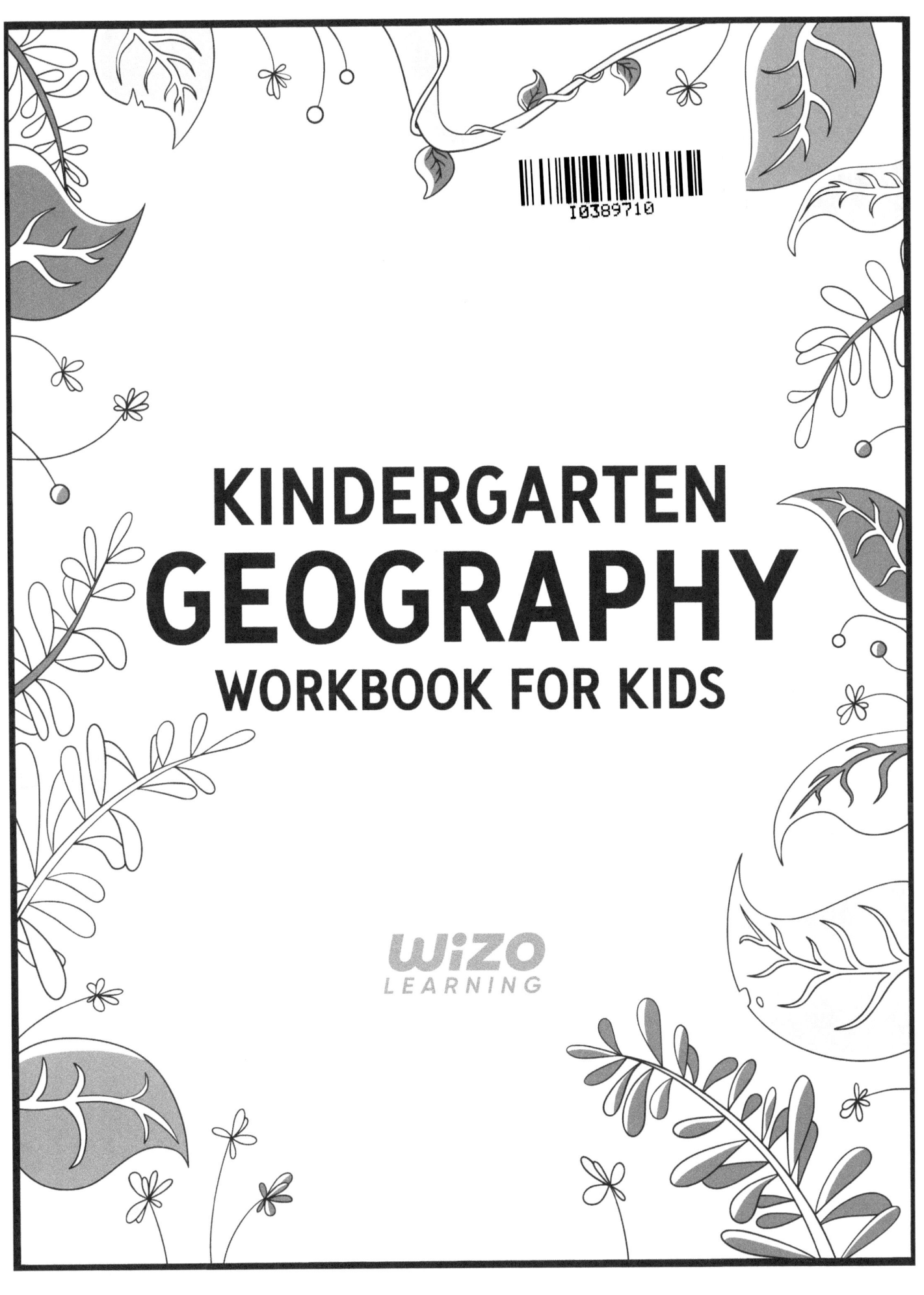

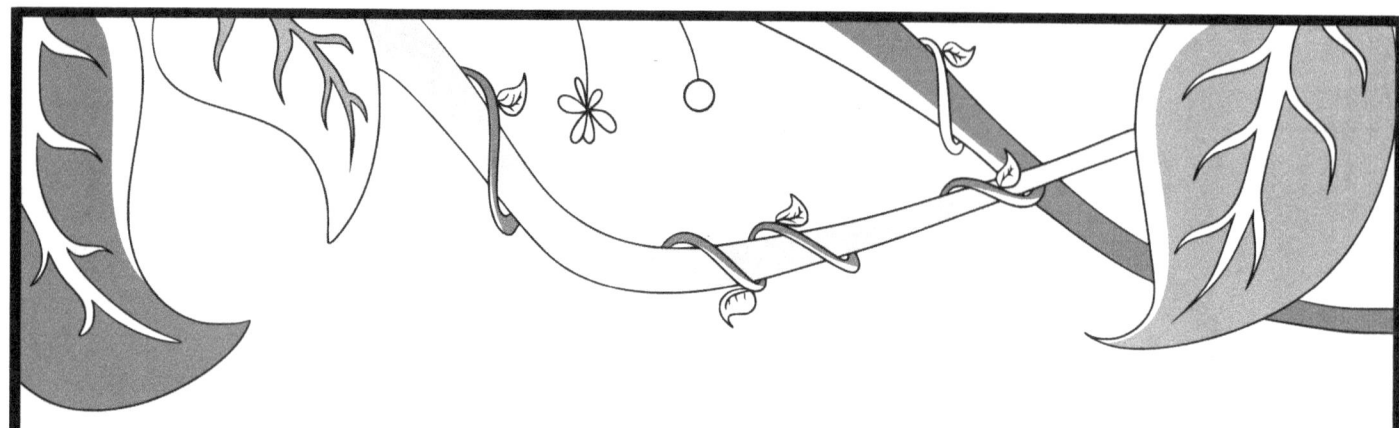

Please consider writing a review!
Just visit: wizolearning.com/review

Copyright 2020. Wizo Learning.
All Rights Reserved.

No part of this book may be reproduced or transmitted
in any form or by any means, electronic or mechanical, including
photocopying, recording or by any other form without written
permission from the publisher.

Have questions? We want to hear from you!
Email us at: support@wizolearning.com

ISBN: 978-1-951806-37-8

FREE BONUS

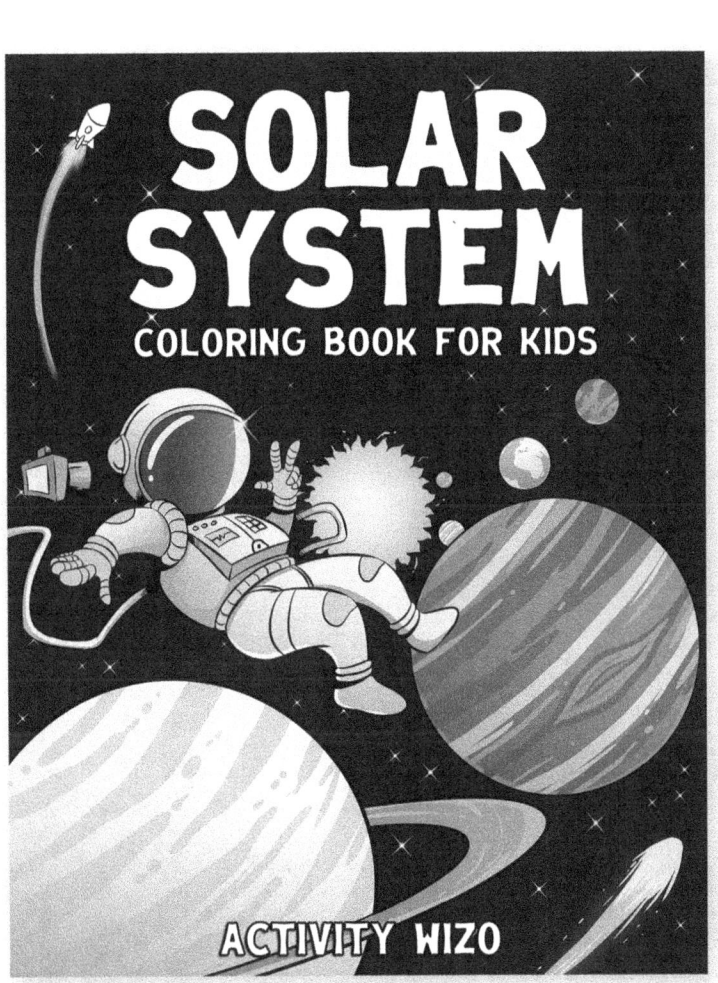

Just visit:
wizolearning.com/solar

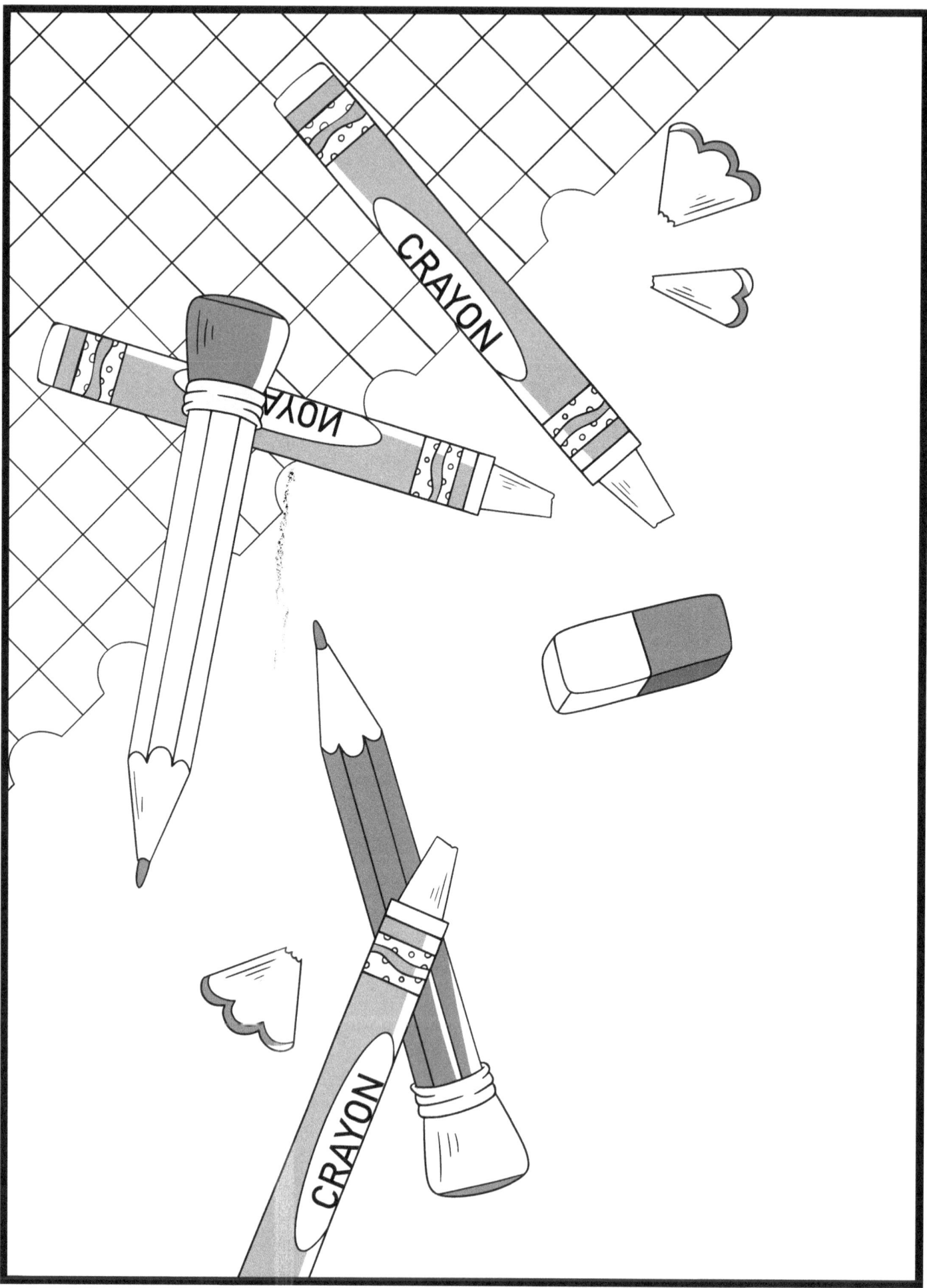

TABLE OF CONTENTS

Chapter 1:	**PLACES**	3
Chapter 2:	**NATURE**	21
Chapter 3:	**WEATHER**	39
Chapter 4:	**PLANTS**	57
Chapter 5:	**ANIMALS**	75
Chapter 6:	**FOOD**	93
Chapter 7:	**PEOPLE**	111
Chapter 8:	**VEHICLES**	129
ANSWER KEY		147

PLACES

The kitchen is where we cook our food. Mark an x over the 5 objects that shouldn't be in the kitchen.

3

PLACES

School is where we study. Draw the other half of the school building.

PLACES

**The playground is where we play with our friends.
Circle the 5 differences between the two playgrounds.**

PLACES

The city is very busy, with lots of people, vehicles, and buildings. Color the objects accordingly.

Red

Blue

Green

Yellow

PLACES

Ryan is going to school. Draw a line from Ryan to the school going through the maze.

PLACES

**School is where we study.
Connect the dots and see what you have drawn.**

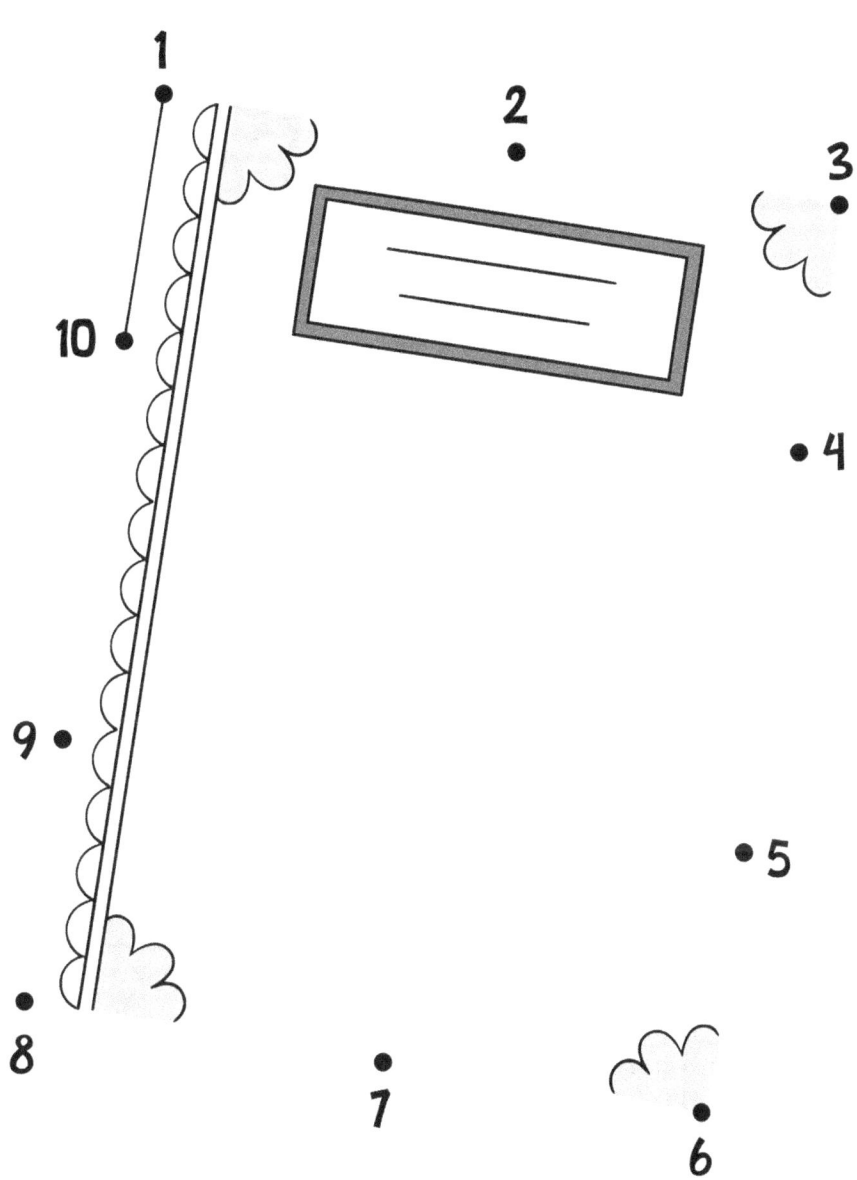

What have you drawn? _____

PLACES

Find these 5 words in the grid:

BOOK   ERASER   PENCIL   PAPER   CHALK

P	A	P	E	R	D	P
S	F	J	H	G	K	E
B	G	L	Y	E	W	N
O	C	H	A	L	K	C
O	X	I	T	R	O	I
K	A	L	P	C	V	L
B	E	R	A	S	E	R

PLACES

The playground is where we play with our friends. Color the objects accordingly.

Red 	Blue 	Pink 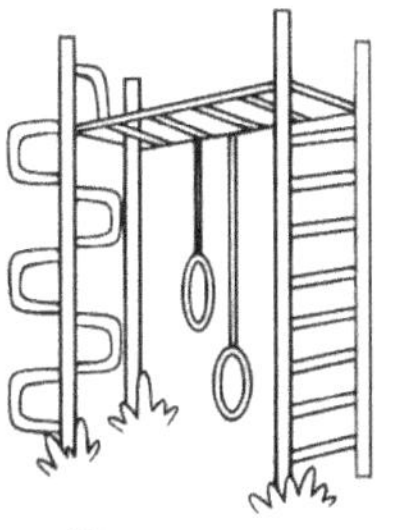	Brown

10

PLACES

Circle the object that is bigger in every comparison.

PLACES

A village is smaller than a town. A city is bigger than both a town and a village. Circle the answer to each question.

Which one has more people?

Which one has taller buildings?

Which one has less people?

12

PLACES

It's fun to play in a playground. Connect the dots and see what you have drawn.

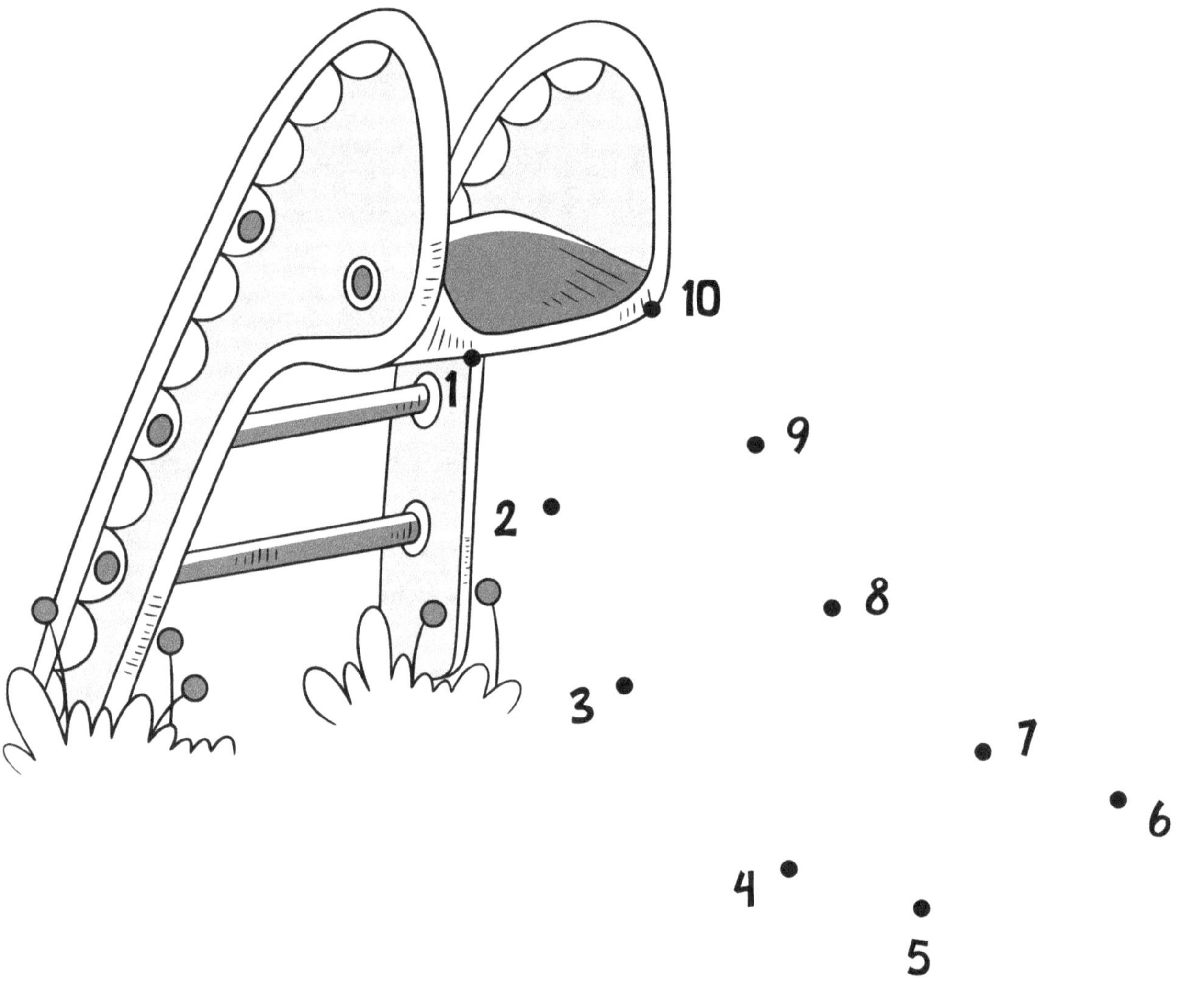

What have you drawn? _____

13

PLACES

**The bedroom is where we sleep.
Circle the 5 differences between the two bedrooms.**

14

PLACES

The bedroom is where we sleep. Mark an x over the 5 objects that shouldn't be in the bedroom.

15

PLACES

Some schools have more students than others.
Circle the answer to each question.

Which school has more students?

Which school is the bigger school?

Which school has less students?

PLACES

Draw a line to connect the objects on the left to the objects on the right.

PLACES

Circle your answers for each question below.

Where do students study?

Where do you find a collection of a lot of books that you can borrow?

Library   /   House   /   Office

Where can you spend your day playing with friends?

Office   /   Library   /   Playground

Which place has more people?

Farm   /   Town   /   City

Where can you find a fire truck?

NATURE

A volcano can erupt and spew hot lava all around it. Draw the other half of a volcano.

NATURE

A lake is a large body of water surrounded by land. Mark an x over the 5 objects that shouldn't be in the lake.

22

NATURE

A forest is a large area covered with trees and undergrowth. Circle the 5 differences between the two forests.

23

NATURE

Find these 5 words in the grid:

HILL　　RIVER　　ROCKS　　VOLCANO　　OCEAN

V	Q	E	L	G	R	H
O	K	N	W	V	T	I
L	O	C	E	A	N	L
C	U	F	Y	D	S	L
A	R	O	C	K	S	Z
N	I	P	O	X	H	J
O	M	R	I	V	E	R

24

NATURE

Maria is going to the log cabin. Draw a line from Maria to the log cabin going through the maze.

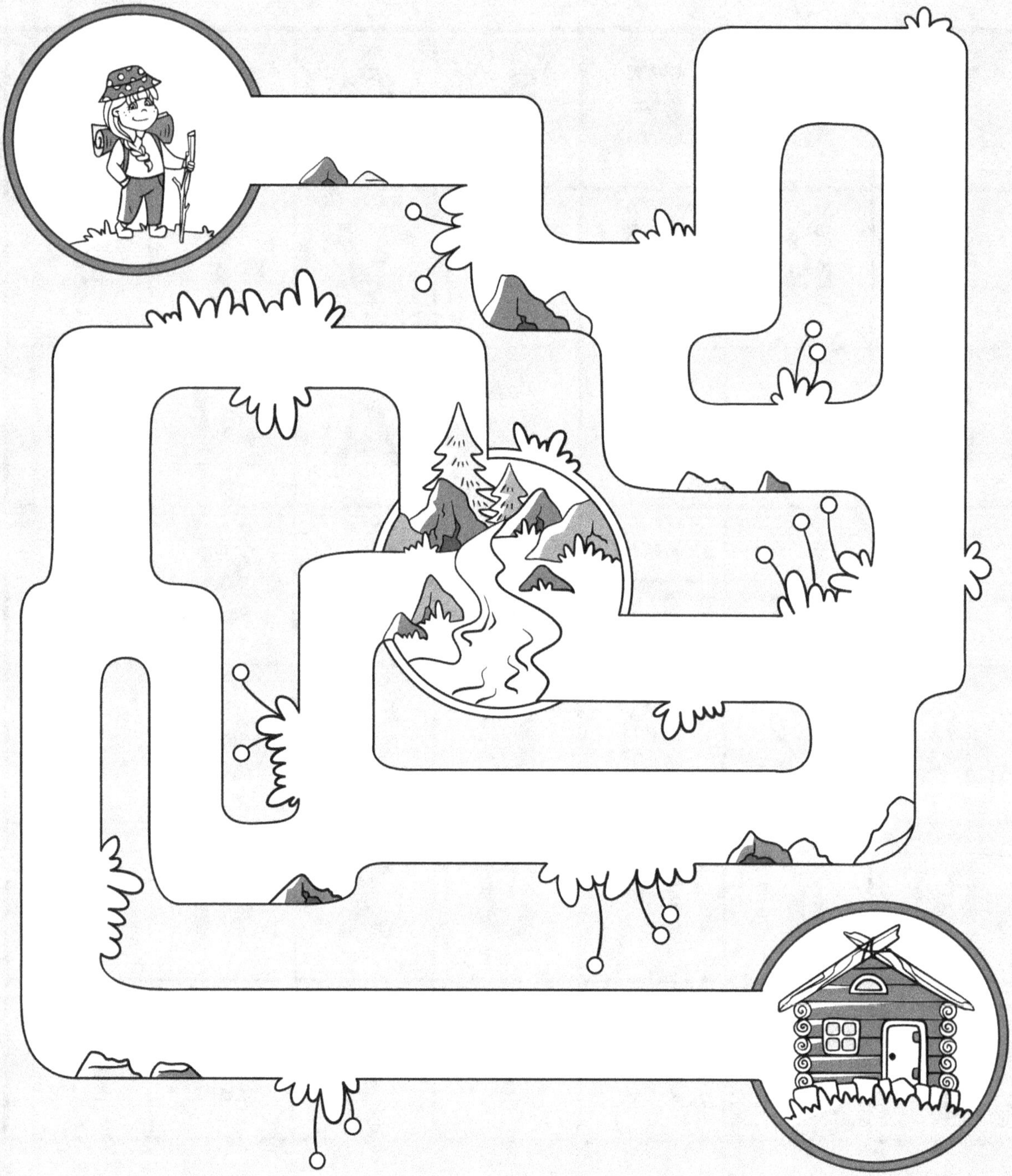

25

NATURE

A pond is smaller than a lake. The ocean is bigger than both a lake and a pond. Circle the answer to each question.

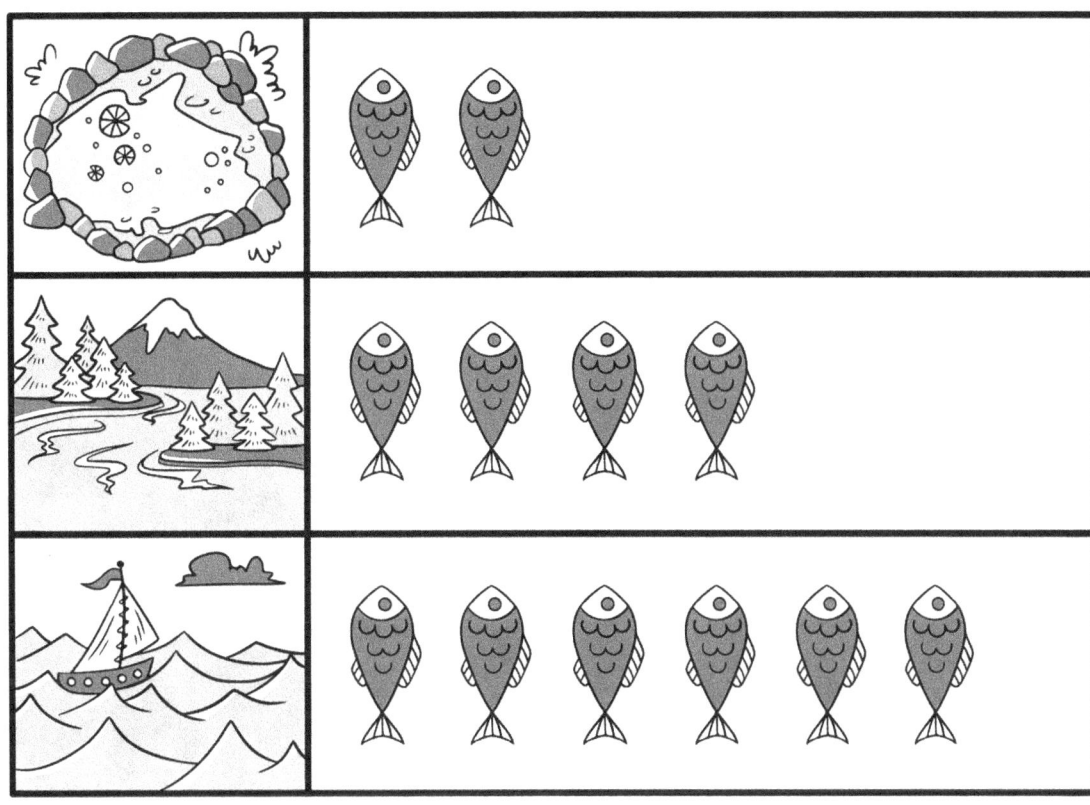

Which one has more fish?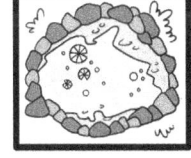

Which one has more water?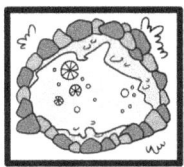

The ocean has more fish than the pond.   TRUE / FALSE

NATURE

A river is a large stream of flowing water.
Mark an x over the 5 objects that shouldn't be in the river.

27

NATURE

A waterfall is water falling from a high river.
Connect the dots and see what you have drawn.

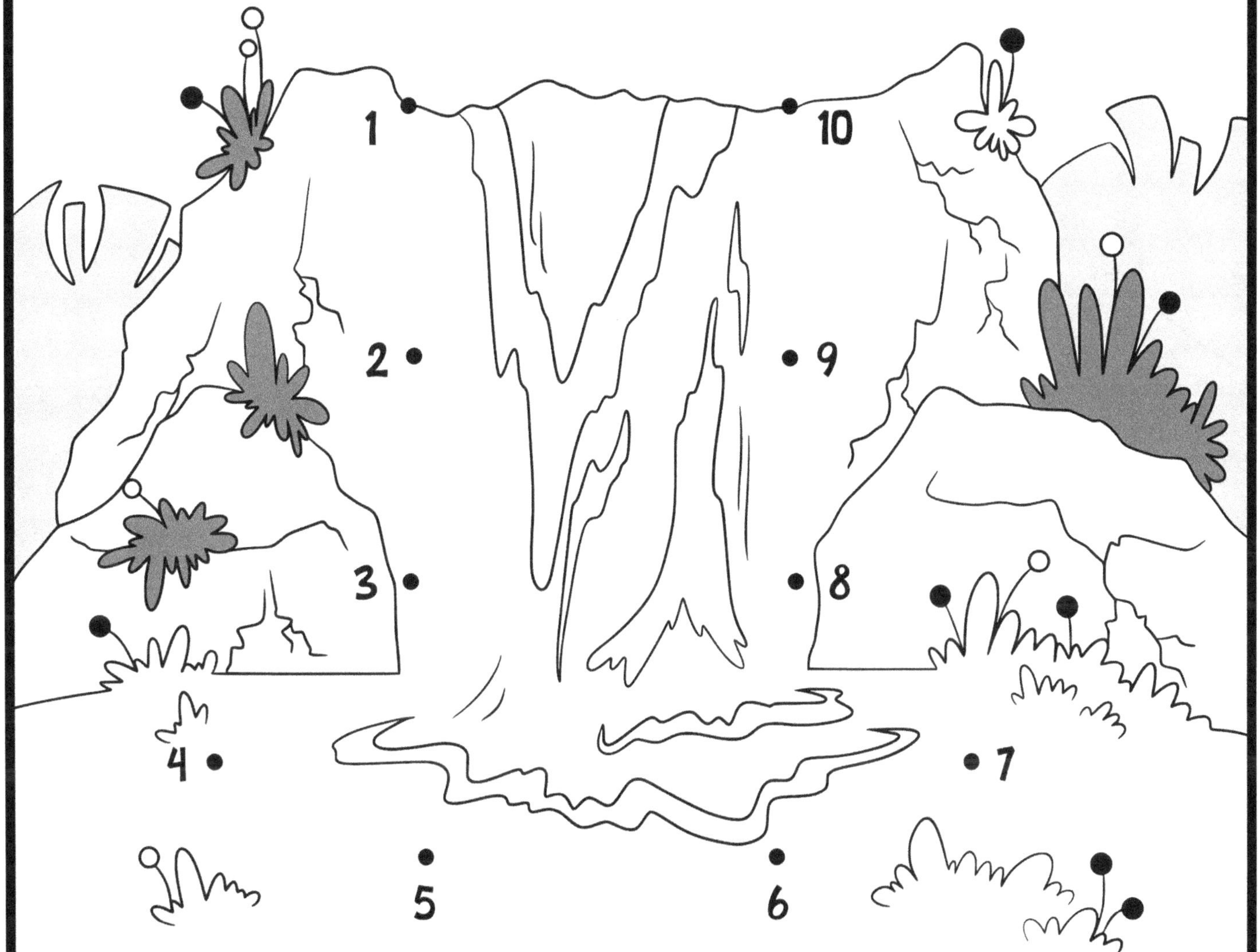

What have you drawn? _____

28

NATURE

A mountain range is a series of mountains lined up. Color the illustration below, according to number.

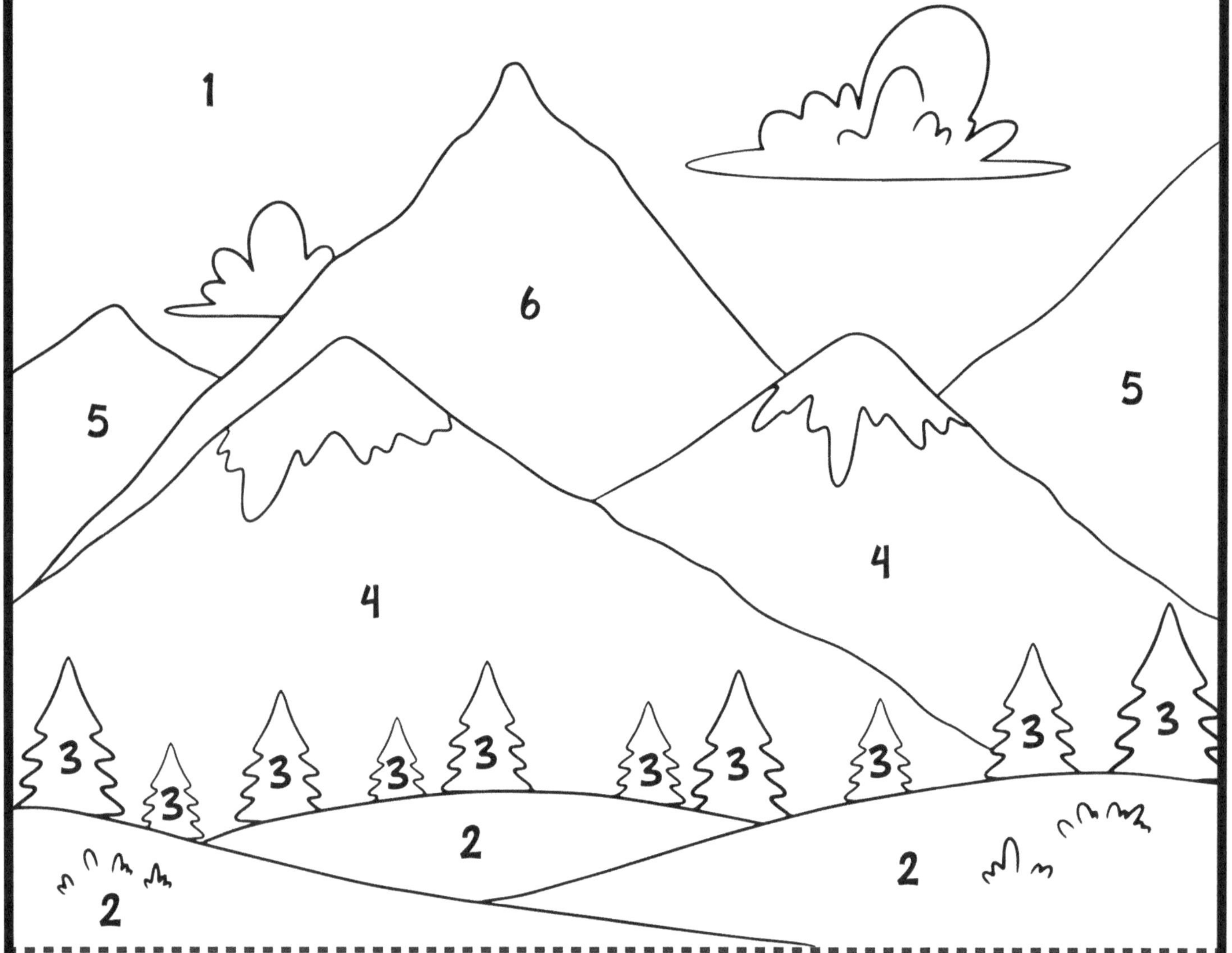

1	BLUE	3	GREEN	5	BROWN
2	LIGHT GREEN	4	ORANGE	6	GRAY

NATURE

Circle what is bigger in every comparison.

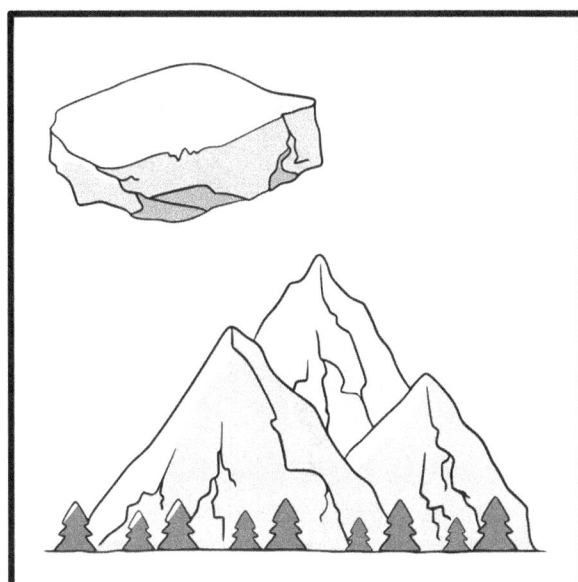

NATURE

Nature is so wonderful. Circle 5 objects that you can see in nature.

31

NATURE

A cabin is where we can stay safely in the woods. Connect the dots and see what you have drawn.

What have you drawn? _____

32

NATURE

A river is a large stream of flowing water.
Circle the 5 differences between the two rivers.

33

NATURE

Draw a line to connect the objects on the left to the words on the right.

Pond

Lake

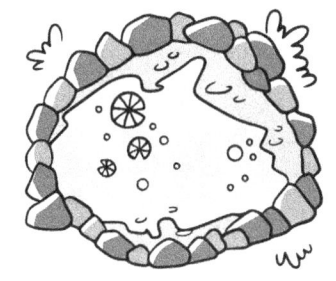

Mountain

Valley

Plain

NATURE

Nature is so wonderful. Circle 5 objects that you can see in nature.

35

NATURE

Circle your answers for each question below.

Which one is the largest body of water?

Pond   /   Lake   /   Ocean

Where can you find a lot of tall trees?

Forest   /   Desert   /   Grassland

Which one spews out hot magma when it erupts?

Where can you find sharks and whales?

Ocean   /   River   /   Savannah

Which one has flowing water?

Lake   /   River   /   Valley

Chapter 3
WEATHER

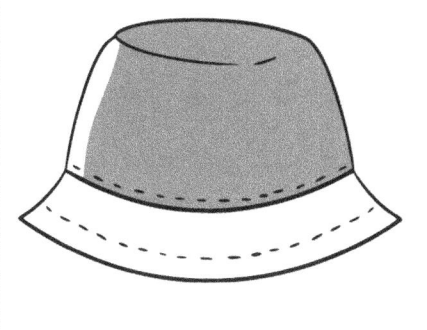

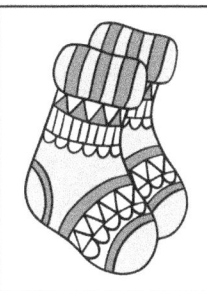

WEATHER

When it's raining, it's best to bring an umbrella. Connect the dots and see what you have drawn.

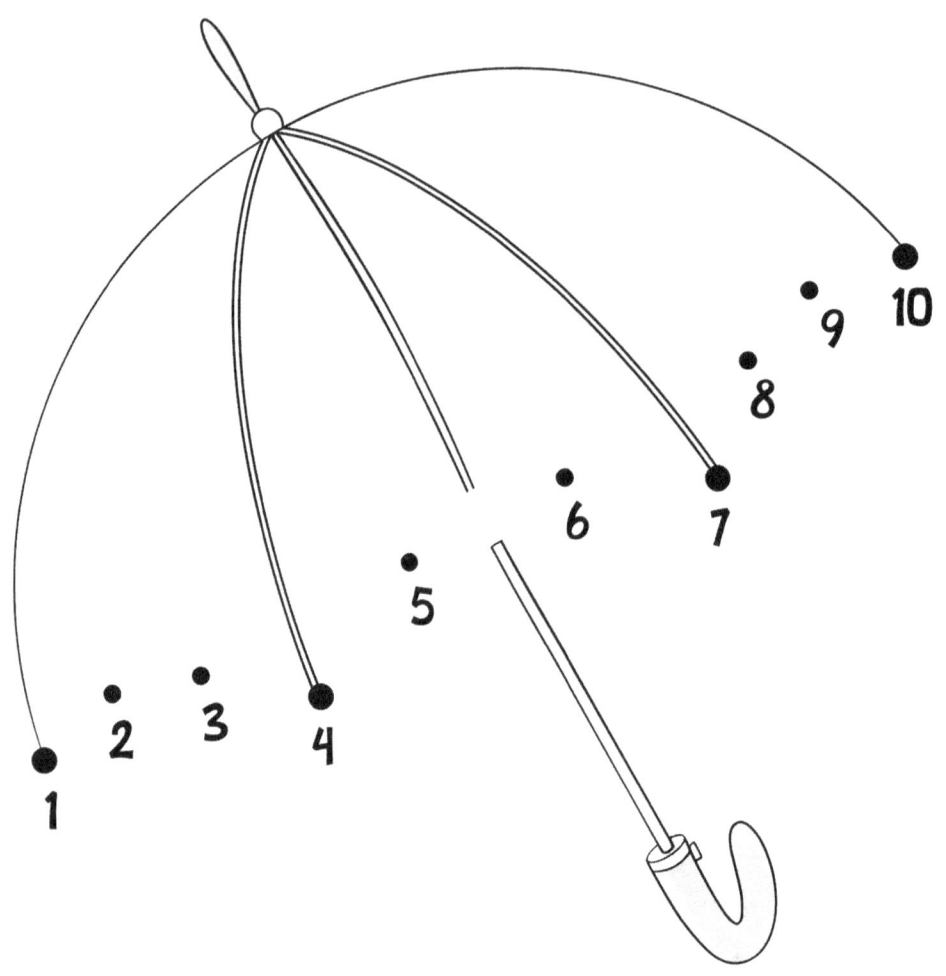

What have you drawn? _____

39

WEATHER

Sometimes it's better to stay inside when it's snowing. Color the illustration below, according to number.

| 1 | BLUE | 3 | YELLOW | 5 | GREEN |
| 2 | DARK GREEN | 4 | BROWN | 6 | RED |

WEATHER

Rainy days aren't always as fun as sunny days. Mark an x over the 5 objects that shouldn't be outside in the rain.

41

WEATHER

We always have a Christmas tree during Christmas. Draw the other half of the Christmas tree.

42

WEATHER

When it rains, you better use these 5 items.
Circle 5 items that you can use when it's raining.

WEATHER

A park is a large green area used for recreation. Circle the 5 differences between the two parks.

44

WEATHER

An umbrella is very useful when it rains. Mark an x over the 5 big umbrellas you can see in the image below.

WEATHER

Better not get wet when it's raining. Circle the object that you can use during the rainy season.

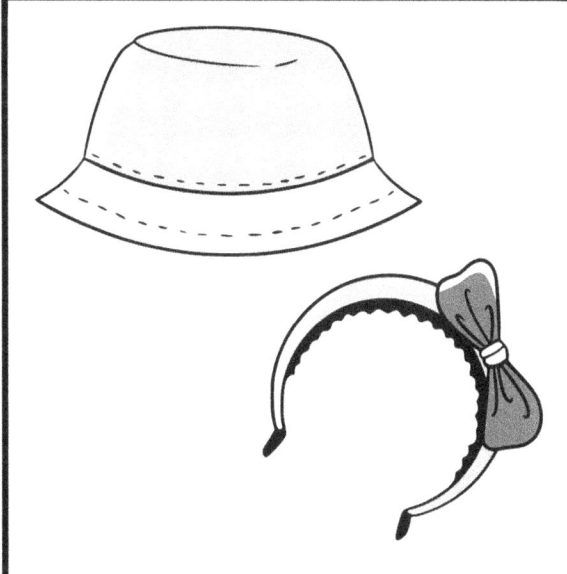

WEATHER

It's great to have fun in the snow. Connect the dots and see what you have drawn.

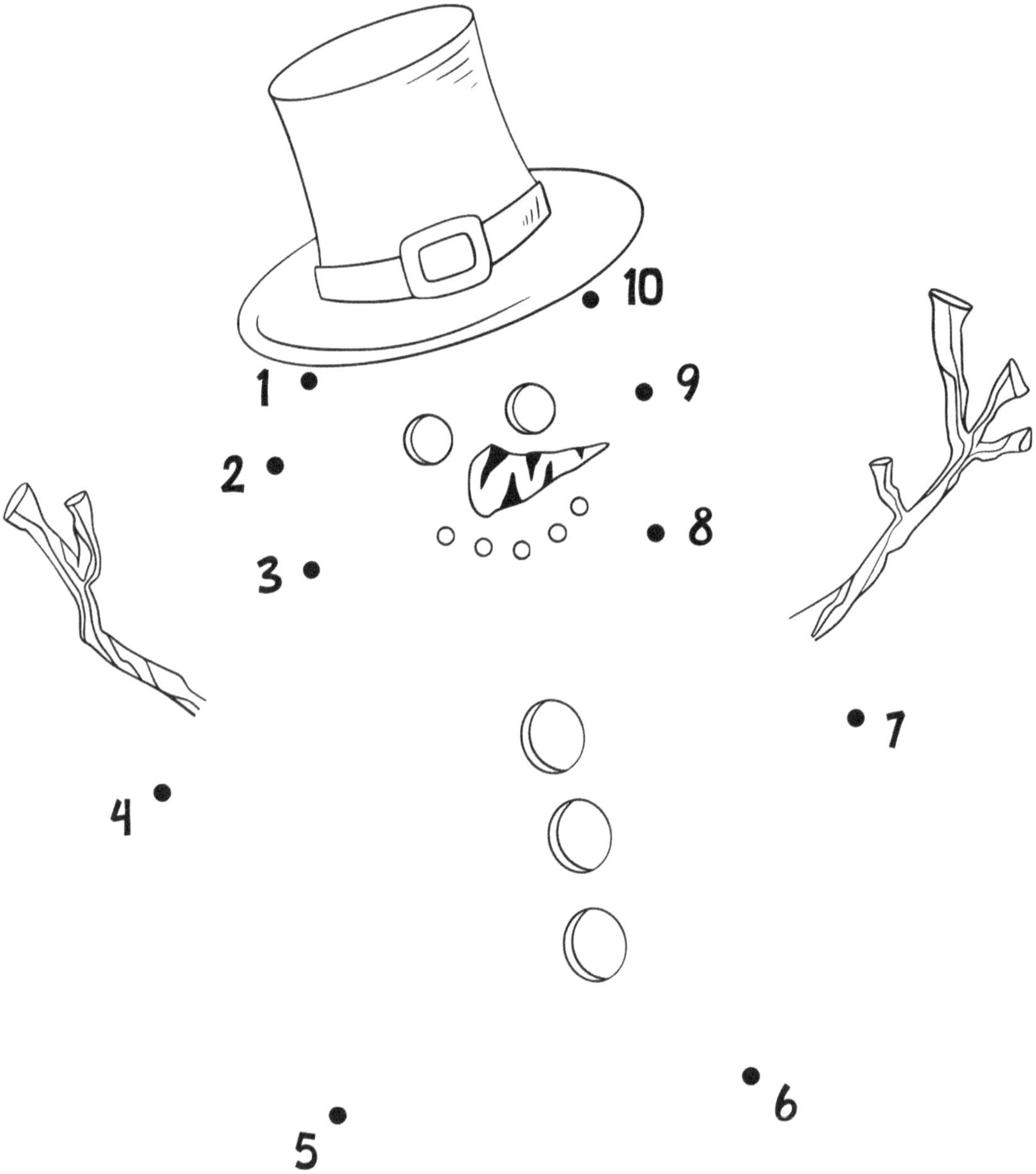

What have you drawn? _____

WEATHER

A park is a large green area used for recreation. Color the illustration below, according to number.

| 1 | BLUE | 3 | DARK GREEN | 5 | PINK |
| 2 | YELLOW | 4 | GREEN | 6 | BROWN |

48

WEATHER

It's really cold when it snows. Circle the 5 differences between the two cities covered in snow.

49

WEATHER

It's really cold when it snows.
Circle **5** objects that you can use when it's snowing.

50

WEATHER

The weather changes all year long. Draw a line to connect the symbols on the left to the words on the right.

   Snowy

   Rainy

   Dry

   Sunny

   Windy

WEATHER

Henry needs to go to work but it's raining. Draw a line from Henry to his umbrella going through the maze.

WEATHER

Find these 5 words in the grid:

SUMMER　　WINTER　　SPRING　　AUTUMN　　SEASON

A	U	T	U	M	N	V
S	L	V	I	E	J	H
E	D	N	A	L	C	R
A	S	P	R	I	N	G
S	Y	L	H	K	X	Q
O	S	U	M	M	E	R
N	W	I	N	T	E	R

53

WEATHER

Circle your answers for each question below.

Which one is part of the four seasons?

Rainy / Winter / Windy

When can you use a raincoat?

Rainy / Sunny / Snowy

Which symbol stands for sunny?

Which one can you build in the snow?

When can you fly a kite?

Windy / Sunny / Raining

Chapter 4
PLANTS

PLANTS

Find these 5 words in the grid:

ACORN   MANGO   ROCK   COCONUT   TREE

U	R	O	C	K	L	D	M
C	O	C	O	N	U	T	R
M	V	J	H	W	P	R	B
A	N	X	R	T	S	E	A
N	Q	I	N	E	D	E	U
G	H	A	C	O	R	N	H
O	R	M	Y	E	V	U	G
M	B	A	J	R	B	Q	E

PLANTS

A rose is a kind of flower, a very beautiful flower. Connect the dots and see what you have drawn.

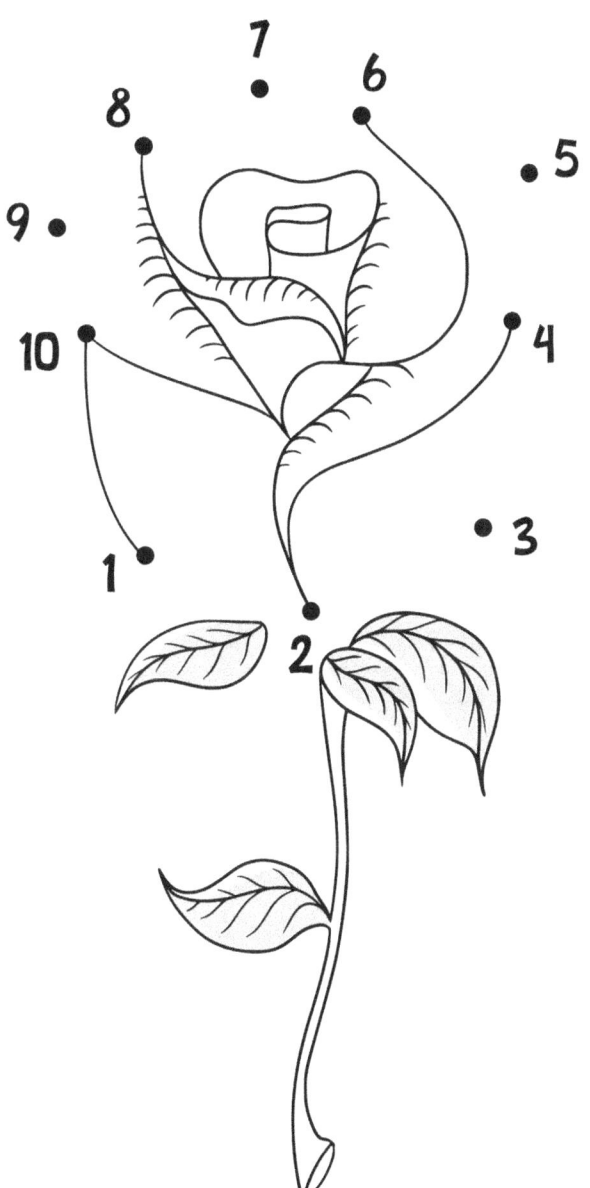

What have you drawn? _____

PLANTS

**An acorn is a type of nut.
Draw the other half of the acorn.**

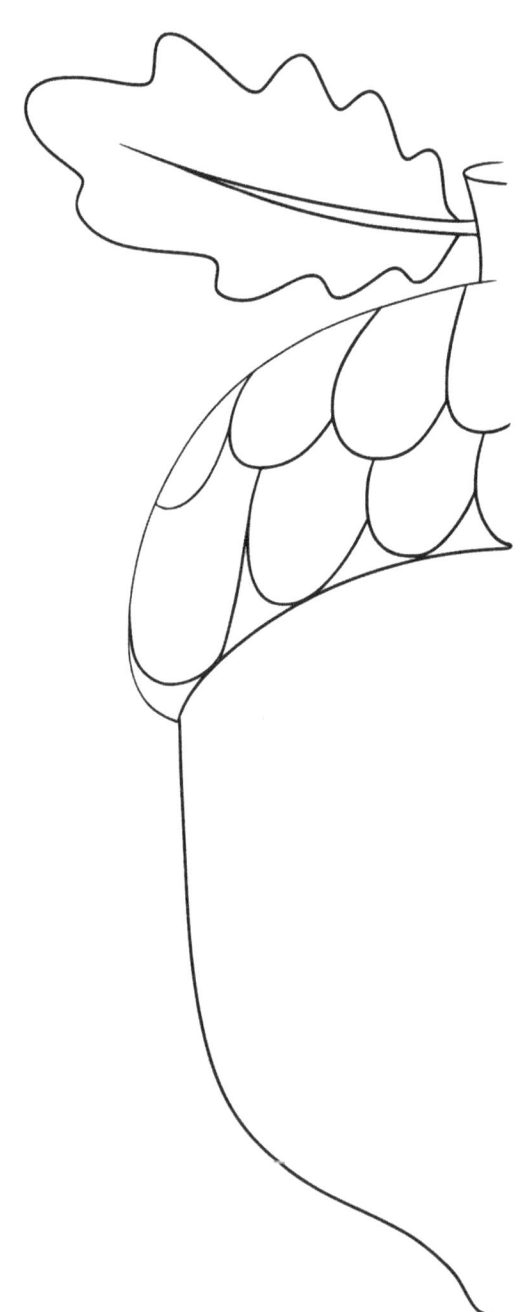

PLANTS

**Some trees have fruits.
Mark an x over the 5 trees that don't bear fruit.**

60

PLANTS

A garden is an open area where you grow plants and flowers. Color the illustration below, according to number.

| 1 | GREEN | 3 | DARK GREEN | 5 | BLUE |
| 2 | BROWN | 4 | ORANGE | 6 | PINK |

PLANTS

**A coconut tree is tall and slender.
Connect the dots and see what you have drawn.**

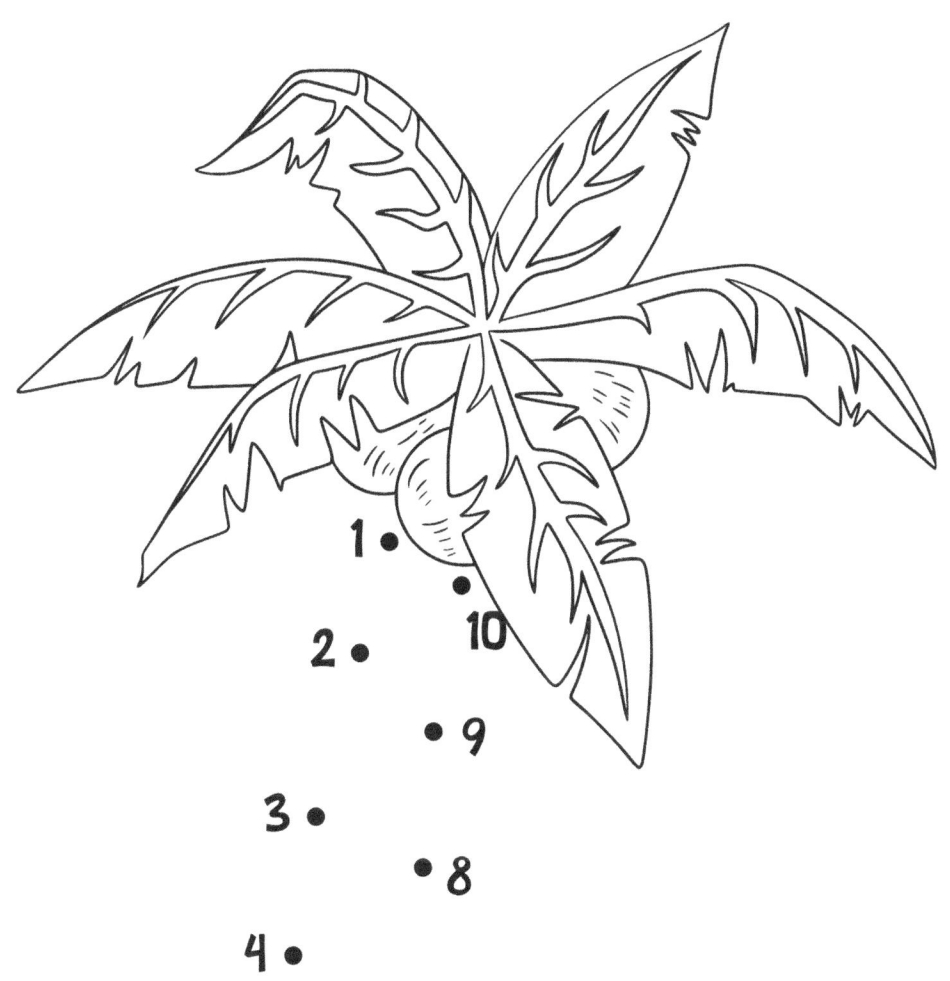

What have you drawn? _____

62

PLANTS

Fruits are delicious and nutritious.
Circle the fruit inside each box.

PLANTS

**Some plants have flowers.
Mark an x over the 5 plants that don't have flowers.**

PLANTS

A greenhouse is a building used to grow plants and flowers. Circle the 5 differences between the two greenhouses.

PLANTS

Mushrooms are not plants.
Circle 5 mushrooms.

PLANTS

Jenny needs to water her sunflower. Draw a line to guide Jenny to the bucket, then to the faucet, then finally to the sunflower, going through the maze.

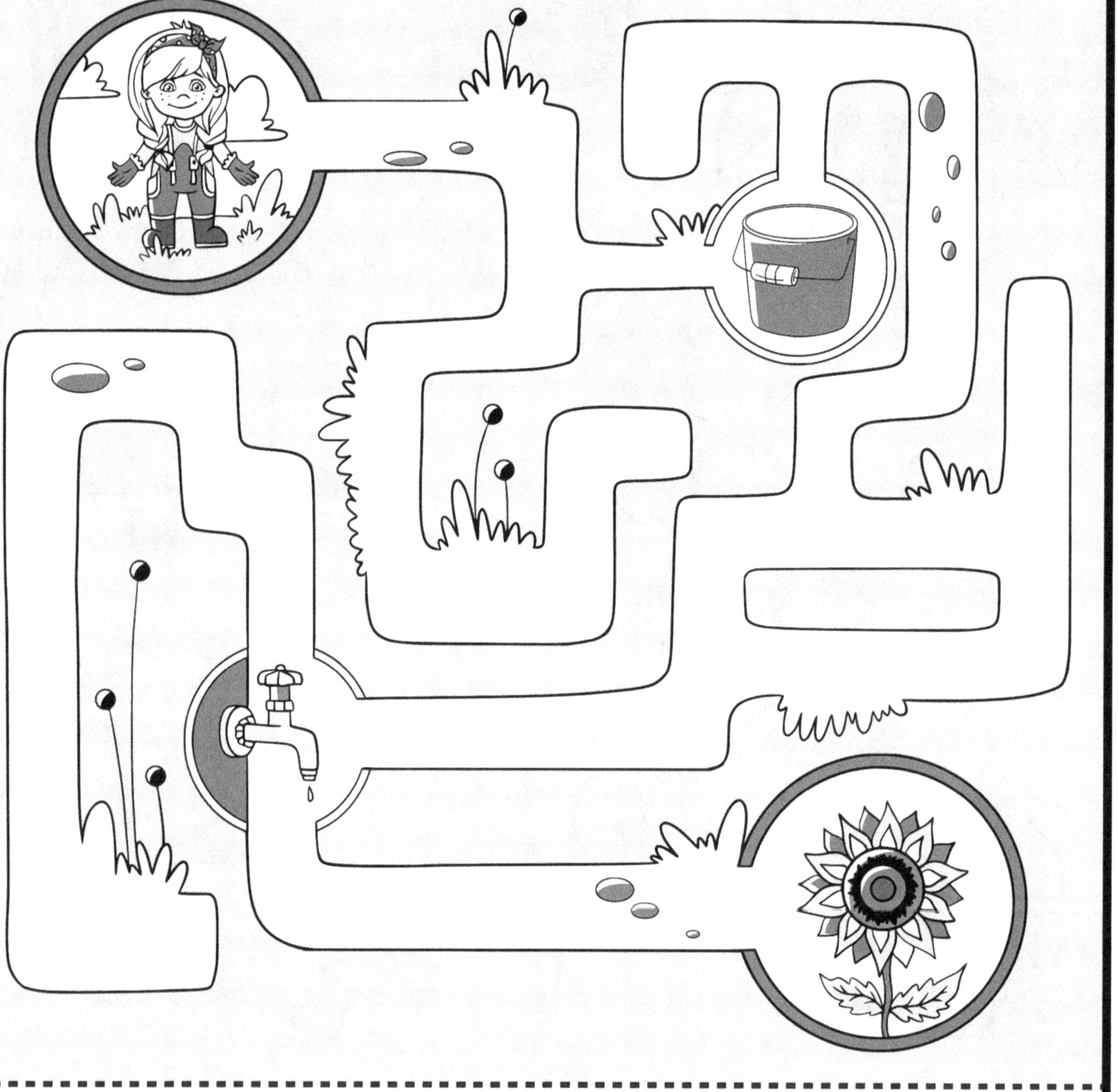

PLANTS

We all need to eat vegetables to grow. Draw a line to connect the vegetables on the left to the words on the right.

   Eggplant

   Potato

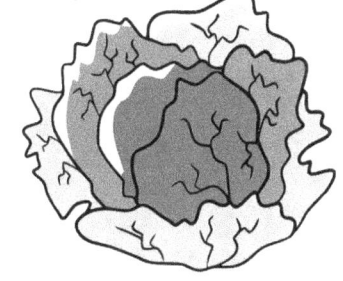   Tomato

   Cabbage

   Carrot

PLANTS

Plants are mostly green with leaves.
Circle 5 plants.

PLANTS

A flower bed is a space in the garden where you grow flowers. Color the illustration below, according to number.

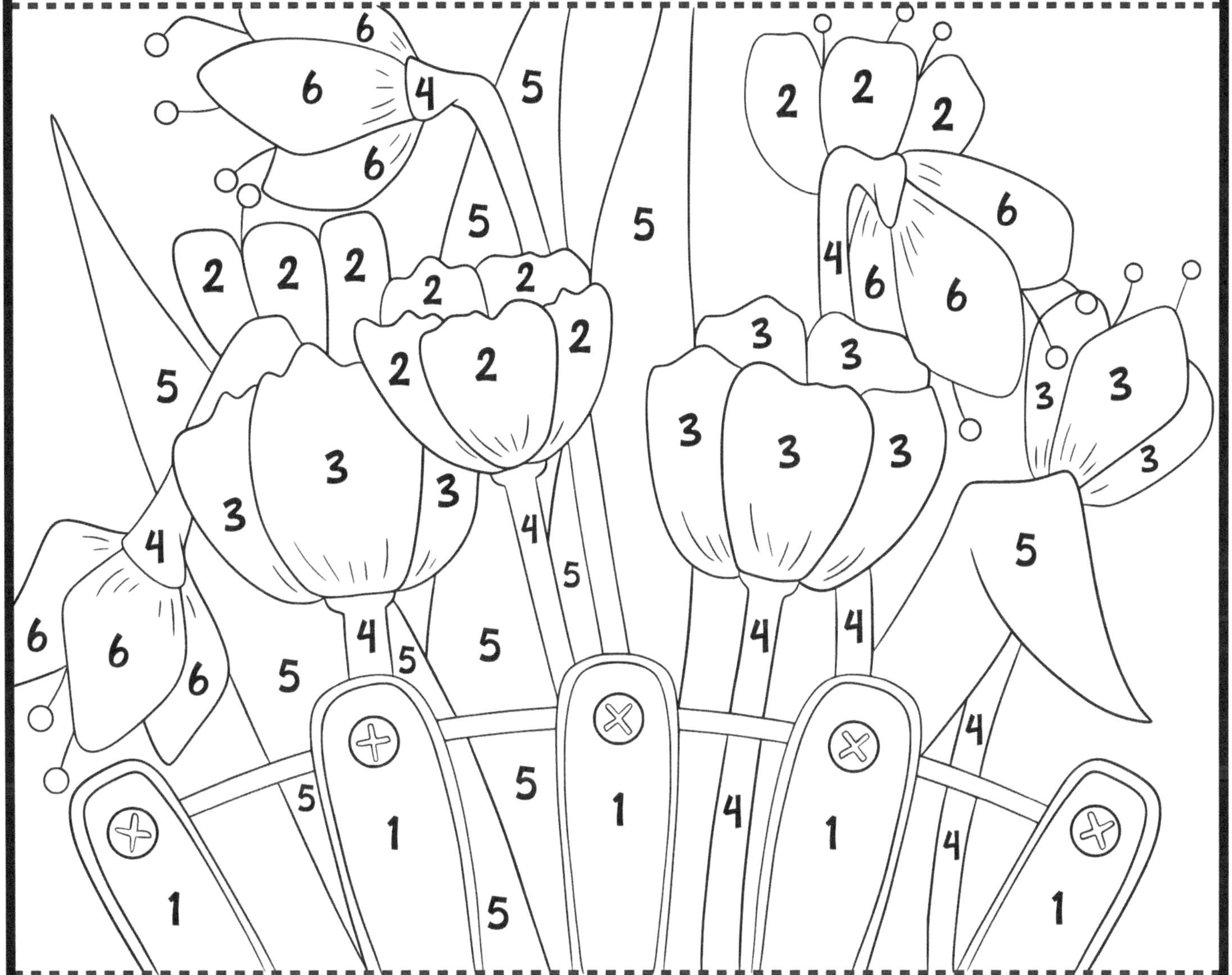

| 1 | BROWN | 3 | PINK | 5 | GREEN |
| 2 | YELLOW | 4 | DARK GREEN | 6 | BLUE |

PLANTS

A forest is a large area covered with trees and undergrowth. Circle the 5 differences between the two forests.

PLANTS

Circle your answers for each question below.

Which one is a fruit?

Which one is a vegetable?

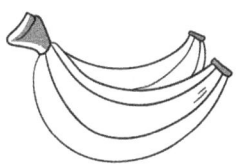 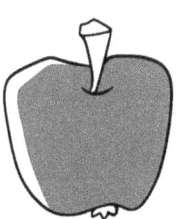 

Which one is the sunflower?

  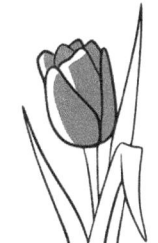

Which one is the biggest?

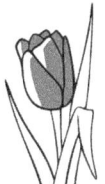  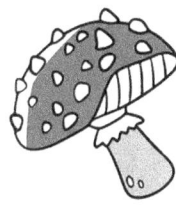

Where can you find a lot of plants and flowers?

Garden   /   Lake   /   River

ANIMALS

Some animals can fly.
Circle 5 animals that can fly.

ANIMALS

Find these 5 words in the grid:

LION   ELEPHANT   GIRAFFE   HORSE   BEAR

G	I	R	A	F	F	E	B
V	D	K	N	Q	H	C	S
L	W	J	L	K	O	L	X
I	Z	U	S	C	R	D	C
O	Y	V	O	X	S	Q	B
N	I	C	M	B	E	A	R
X	V	O	R	O	L	C	D
E	L	E	P	H	A	N	T

ANIMALS

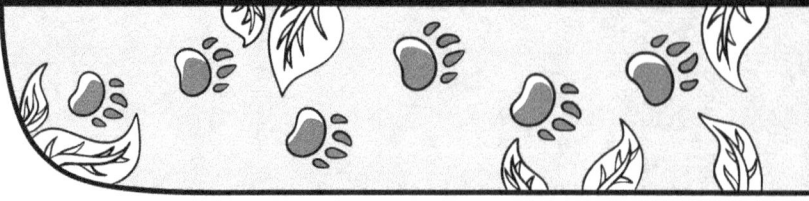

You can find a lot of different kinds of animals in the forest. Circle the 5 differences between the two forests with animals.

77

ANIMALS

A grassland is a large open area of country covered with grass, especially one used for grazing.
Color the illustration below, according to number.

| 1 | DARK GREEN | 3 | YELLOW | 5 | PINK |
| 2 | GREEN | 4 | BROWN | 6 | BLUE |

ANIMALS

**Some animals can fly.
Mark an x over the 5 animals that can fly.**

ANIMALS

**The lion is the king of the jungle.
Draw the other half of the lion's face.**

80

ANIMALS

A farm is where you raise farm animals. Circle the 5 differences between the two farms.

ANIMALS

Some animals are smaller than others. Circle the animal that is smaller in every comparison.

ANIMALS

A farm is where you raise farm animals. Mark an x over the 5 animals that don't belong in a farm.

83

ANIMALS

A bear wants to go home to his cave. Draw a line from the bear to the cave, going through the maze.

84

ANIMALS

Draw a line to connect the body part on the left to the animals on the right.

85

ANIMALS

A zoo is where animals are kept in captivity.
Color the illustration below, according to number.

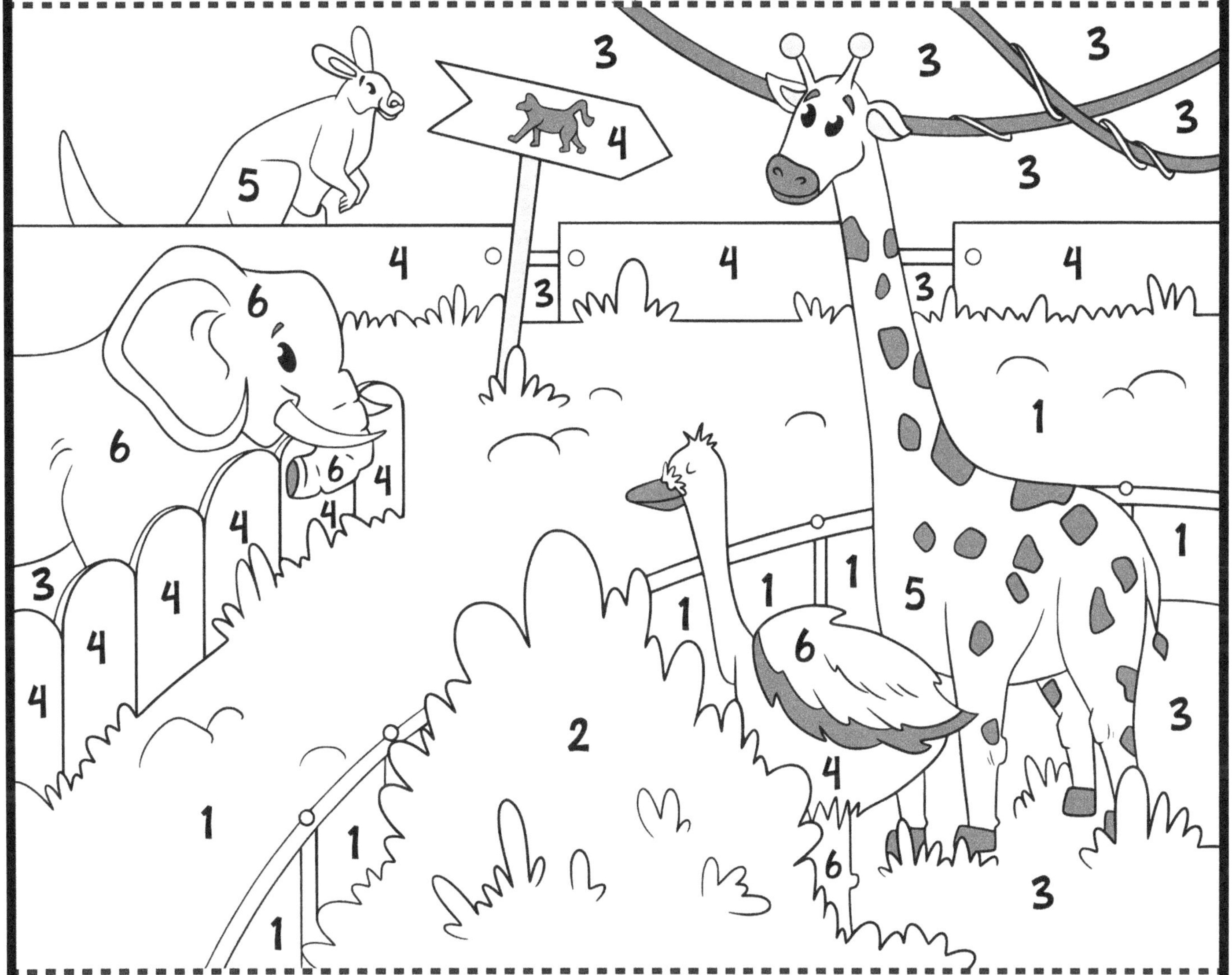

| 1 | YELLOW | 3 | GREEN | 5 | ORANGE |
| 2 | DARK GREEN | 4 | BROWN | 6 | GRAY |

ANIMALS

**Rabbits are cute little creatures.
Connect the dots and see what you have drawn.**

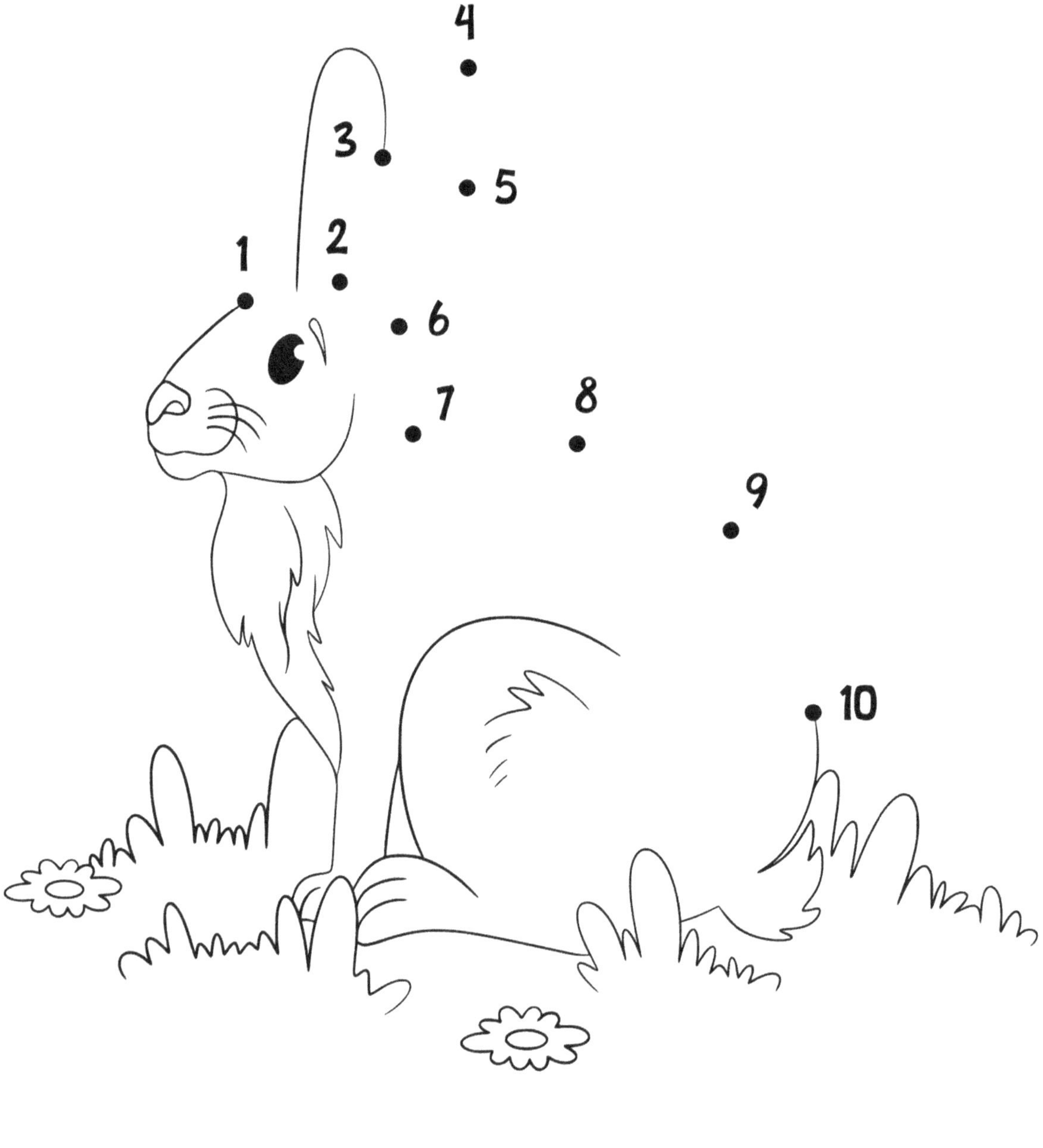

What have you drawn? _____

87

ANIMALS

**Some animals live on land.
Circle 5 animals that live on land.**

ANIMALS

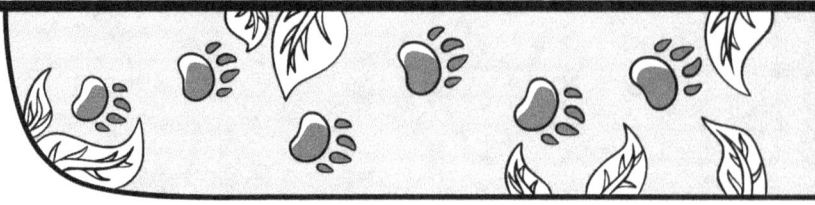

A pig is a kind of farm animal.
Connect the dots and see what you have drawn.

What have you drawn? _____

89

ANIMALS

Circle your answers for each question below.

Which one is a land animal?

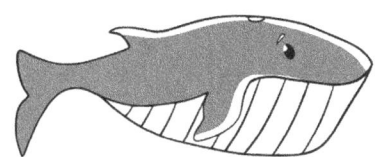  

Which one is the predator?

Which one can lay eggs?

Which one is the biggest?

Where can you find animals in captivity?

Forest / Ocean / Zoo

FOOD

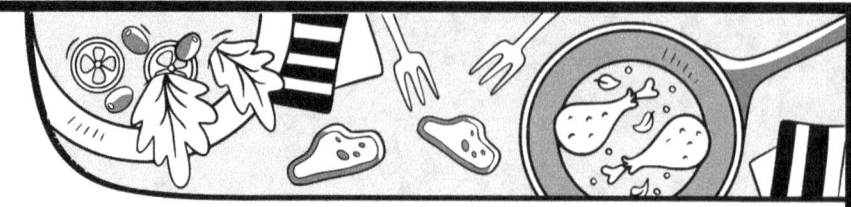

An Italian restaurant is where you can eat Italian food. Color the illustration below, according to number.

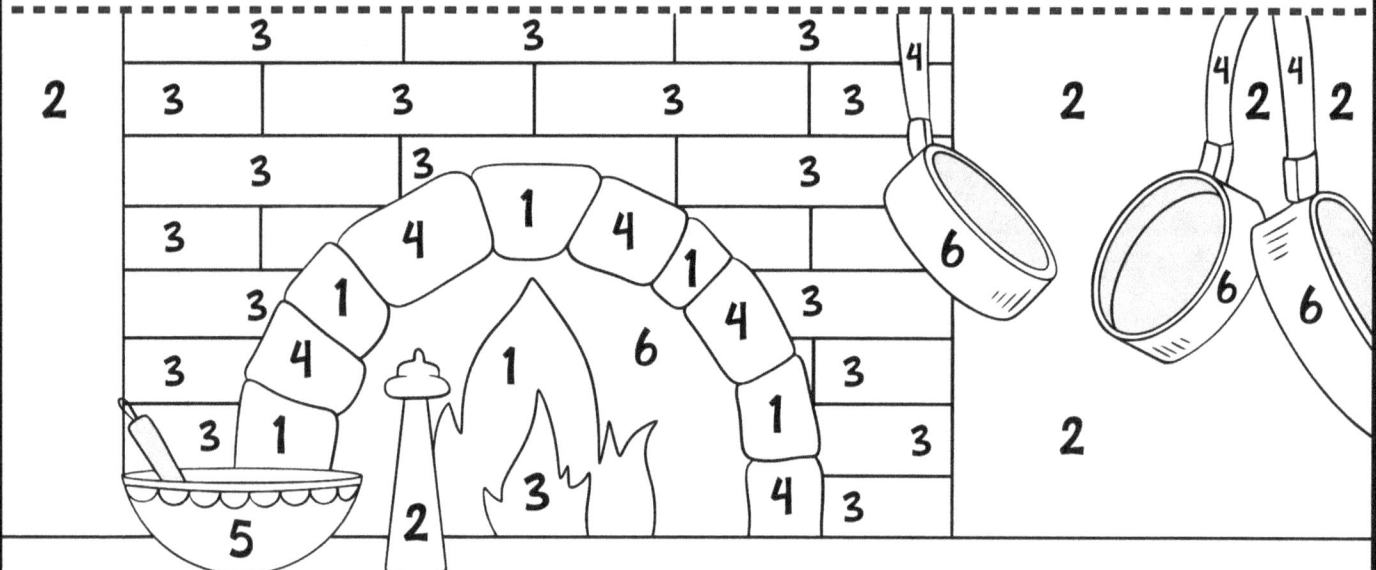

| 1 | RED | 3 | YELLOW | 5 | GREEN |
| 2 | BLUE | 4 | BROWN | 6 | BLACK |

FOOD

Bread is a dough-based food you can bake and eat. Circle 5 types of bread.

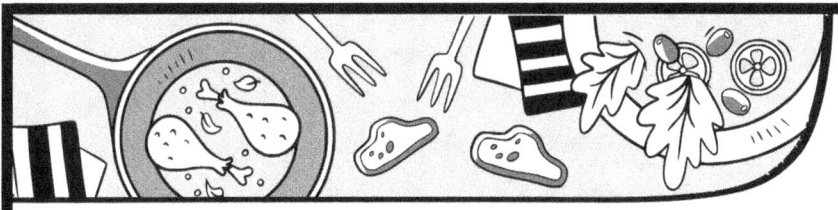

94

FOOD

A food court is a place where there are lots of food choices. Circle the 5 differences between the two food courts.

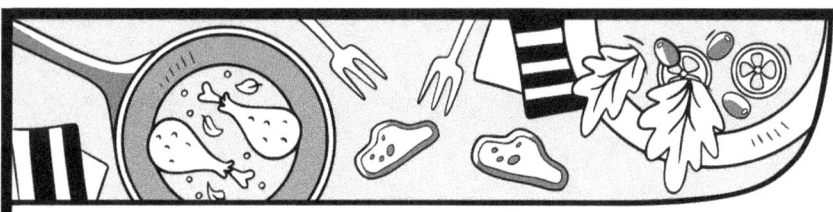

FOOD

A vegetable garden is where you can grow vegetables. Color the illustration below, according to number.

| 1 | BROWN | 3 | GREEN | 5 | PINK |
| 2 | DARK GREEN | 4 | ORANGE | 6 | PURPLE |

FOOD

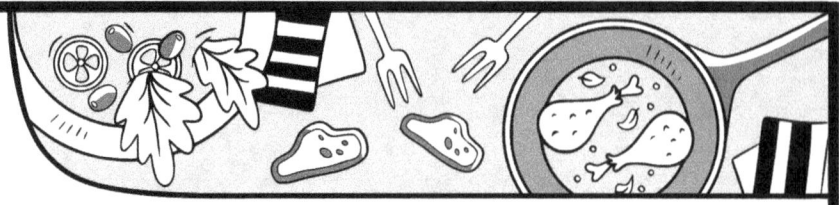

A doughnut is a round dough-based food you can bake and eat. Draw the other half of the doughnut.

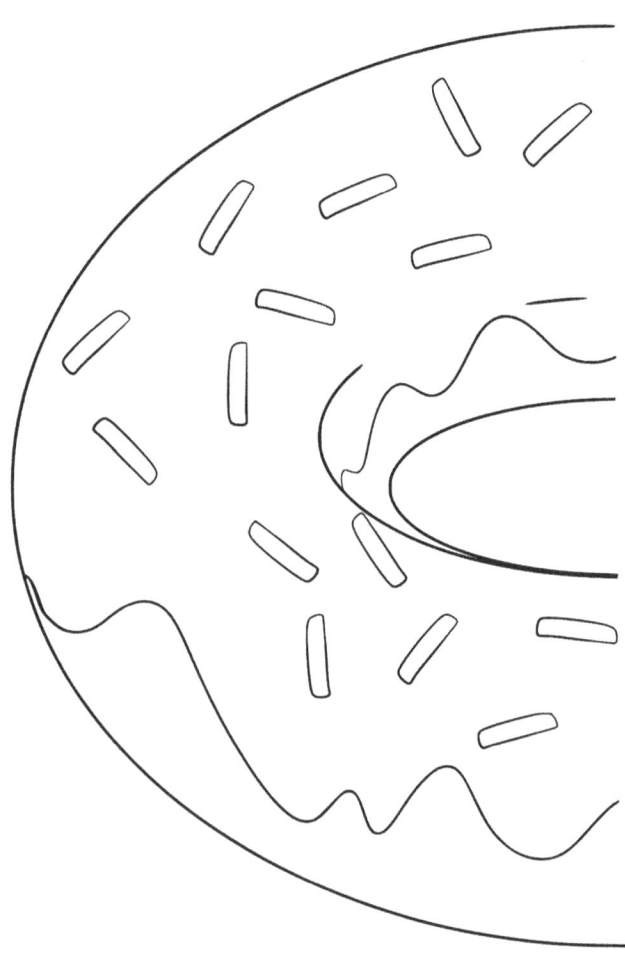

FOOD

There are different flavours of doughnuts. Mark an x over the 5 types of food that don't belong to a doughnut shop.

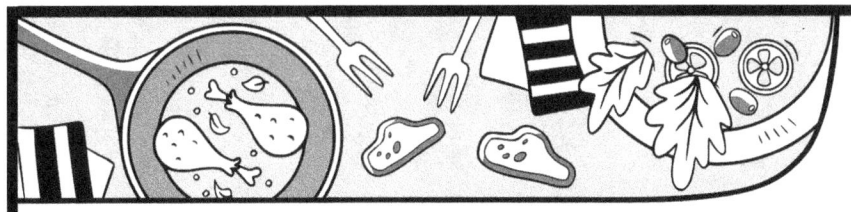

FOOD

We eat dinner at the dinner table.
Circle the 5 differences between the two dinner tables.

99

FOOD

**There are different shapes of pasta.
Circle 5 types of pasta.**

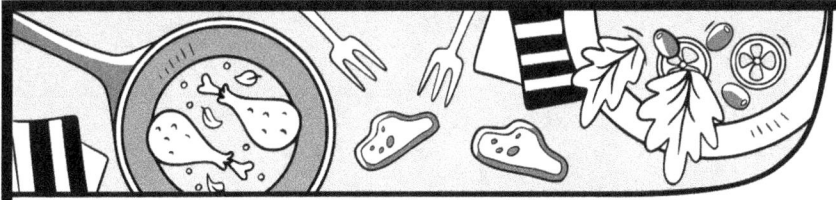

100

FOOD

A fruit stand is where you can find and buy all kinds of fruits. Mark an x over the 5 types of food that don't belong to a fruit stand.

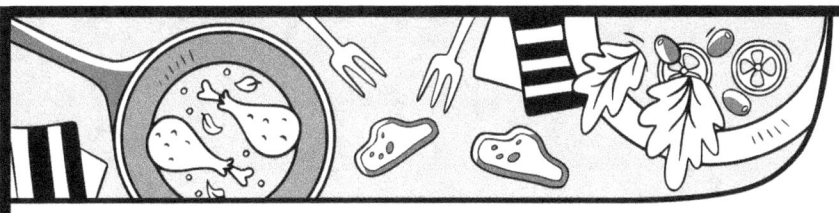

FOOD

Draw a line to connect the utensil on the left to the food on the right.

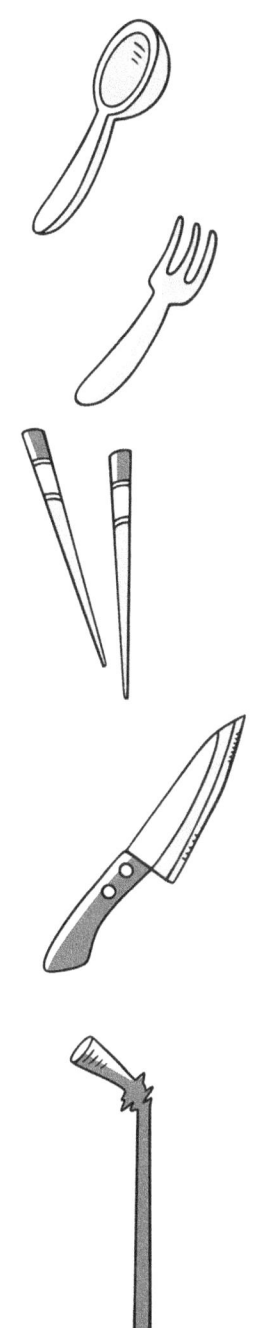

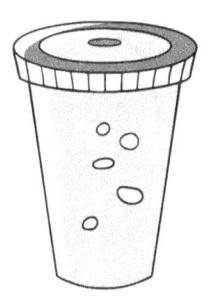

102

FOOD

The meatballs need to be on the spaghetti. Draw a line from the meatballs to the spaghetti, going through the maze.

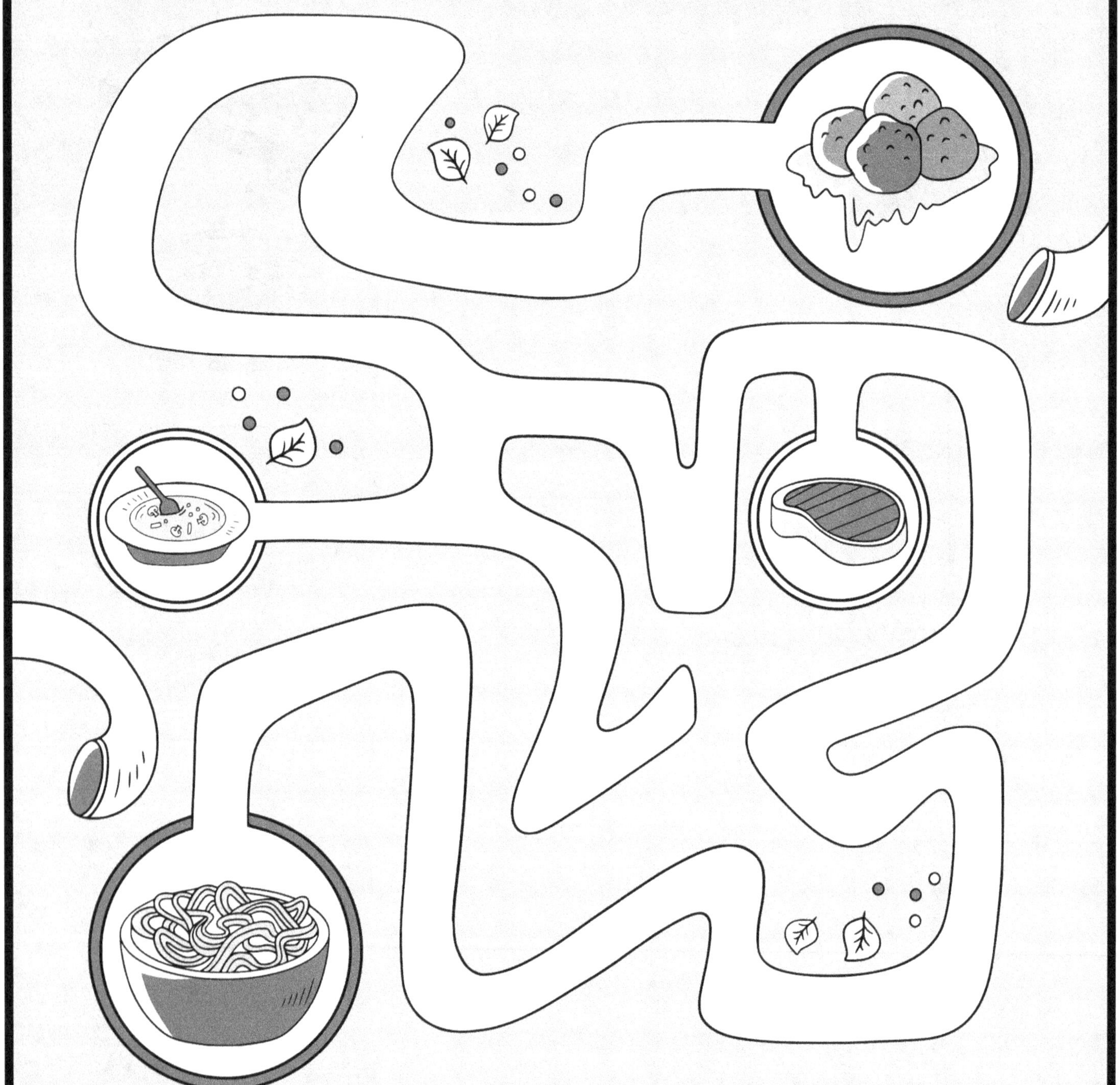

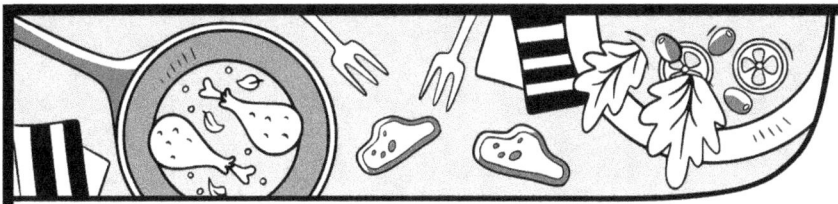

FOOD

We use different kinds of utensils for eating. Circle the utensil inside each box.

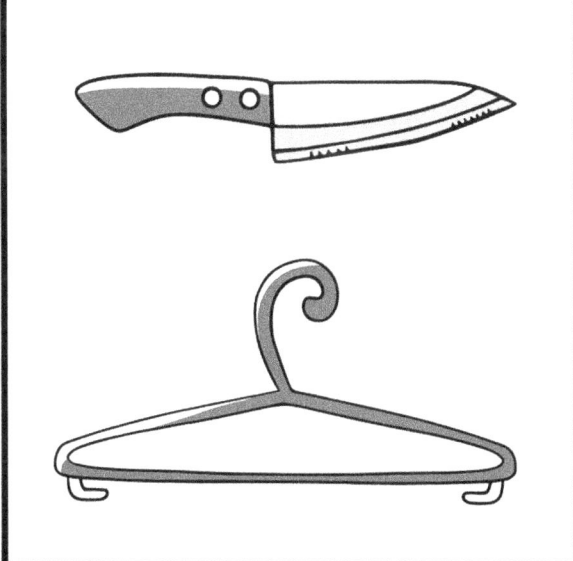

FOOD

We use a cooking pot to cook our food.
Connect the dots and see what you have drawn.

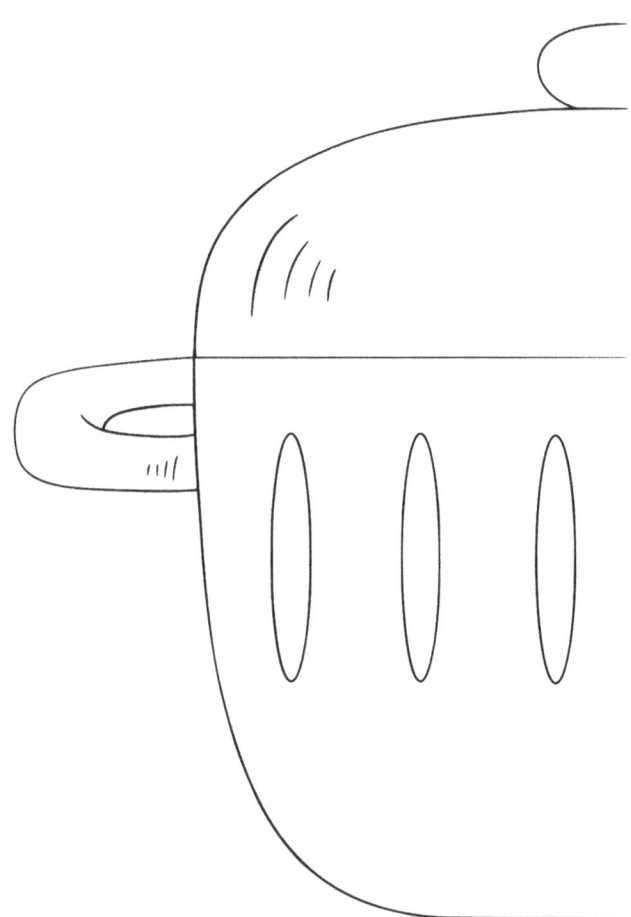

What have you drawn? _____

105

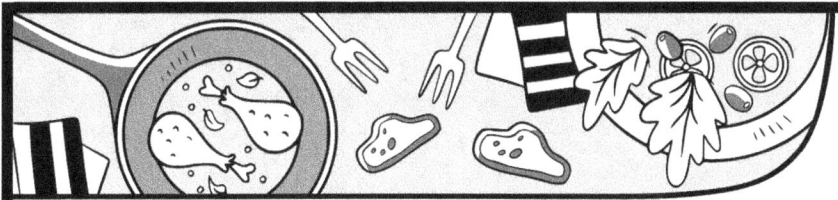

FOOD

Find these 5 words in the grid:

SPAGHETTI   DOUGHNUT   BREAD   CUCUMBER   SPOON

F	S	X	C	F	A	B	X	L	R
S	P	O	O	N	H	R	C	U	K
K	A	C	E	I	L	C	V	S	C
Q	G	L	W	V	D	L	U	I	E
R	H	O	S	R	H	Q	G	B	D
L	E	V	O	L	H	J	H	R	S
N	T	C	U	C	U	M	B	E	R
Z	T	X	E	Y	X	U	X	A	Y
V	I	A	O	C	D	R	S	D	H
D	O	U	G	H	N	U	T	Y	V

FOOD

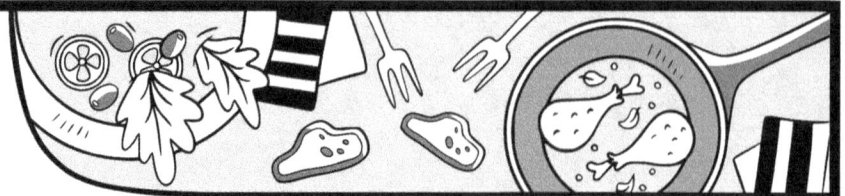

A refrigerator is where we store our food to eat for later. Connect the dots and see what you have drawn.

What have you drawn? _____

107

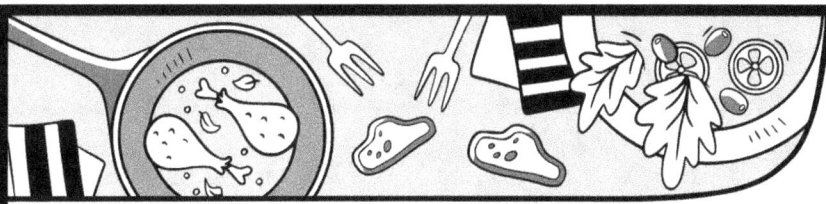

FOOD

Circle your answers for each question below.

In what country does spaghetti come from?

Japan   /   Italy   /   Australia

What utensil do you use to eat soup?

Which one is a kind of pasta?

Which one is made out of potatoes?

Where can you pay for food to eat?

Office   /   Police Station   /   Restaurant

PEOPLE

Police officers keep us safe from bad people. Circle the 5 differences between the two Police Officers.

PEOPLE

The doctor needs to attend to her patient. Draw a line from the doctor to the patient, going through the maze.

PEOPLE

A hospital is where we get treated for different kinds of illnesses. Color the illustration below, according to number.

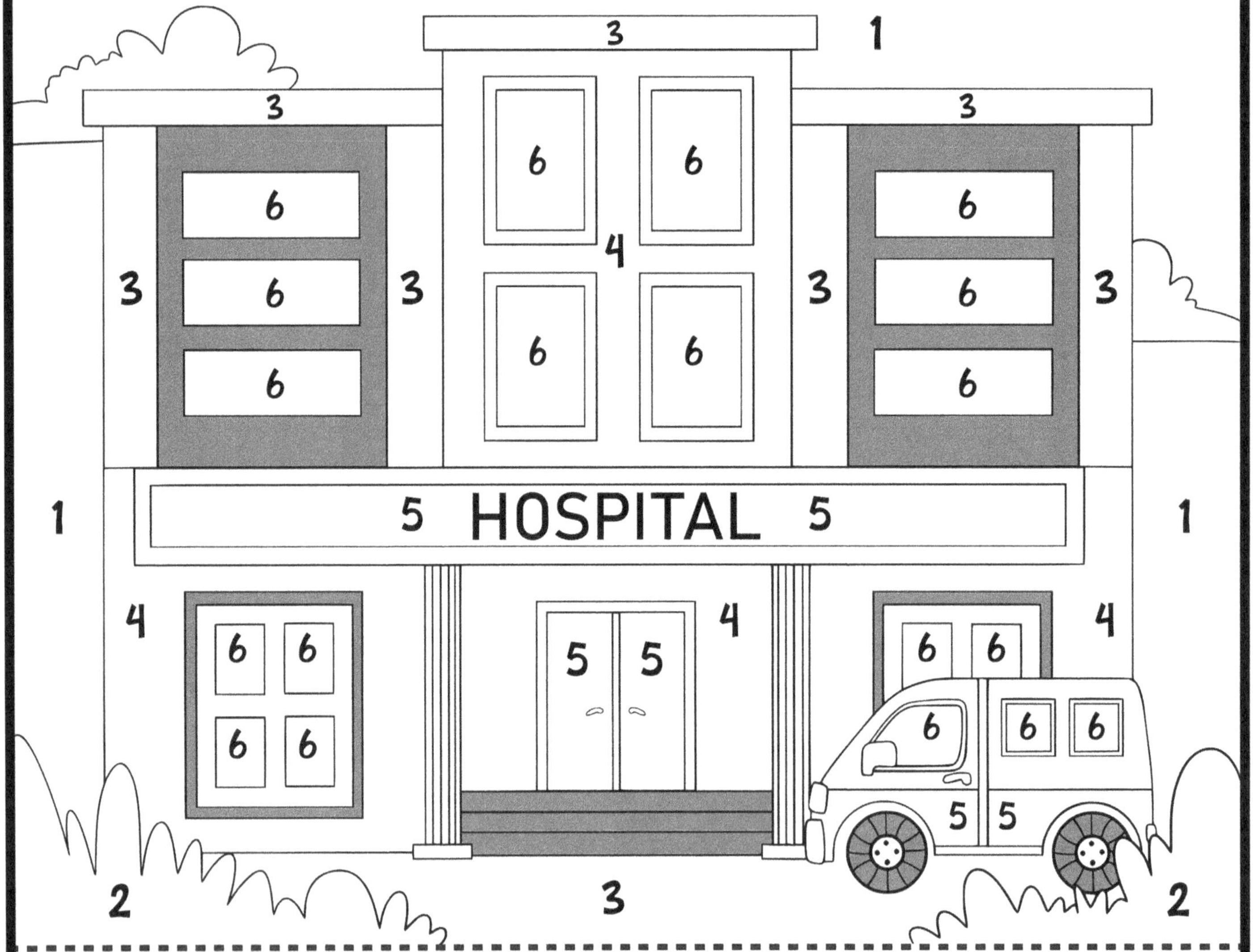

| 1 | BLUE | 3 | BROWN | 5 | RED |
| 2 | GREEN | 4 | YELLOW | 6 | LIGHT BLUE |

PEOPLE

Our military protects our country.
Circle 5 persons in military uniform.

114

PEOPLE

**A doctor is someone who treats our sickness.
Connect the dots and see what you have drawn.**

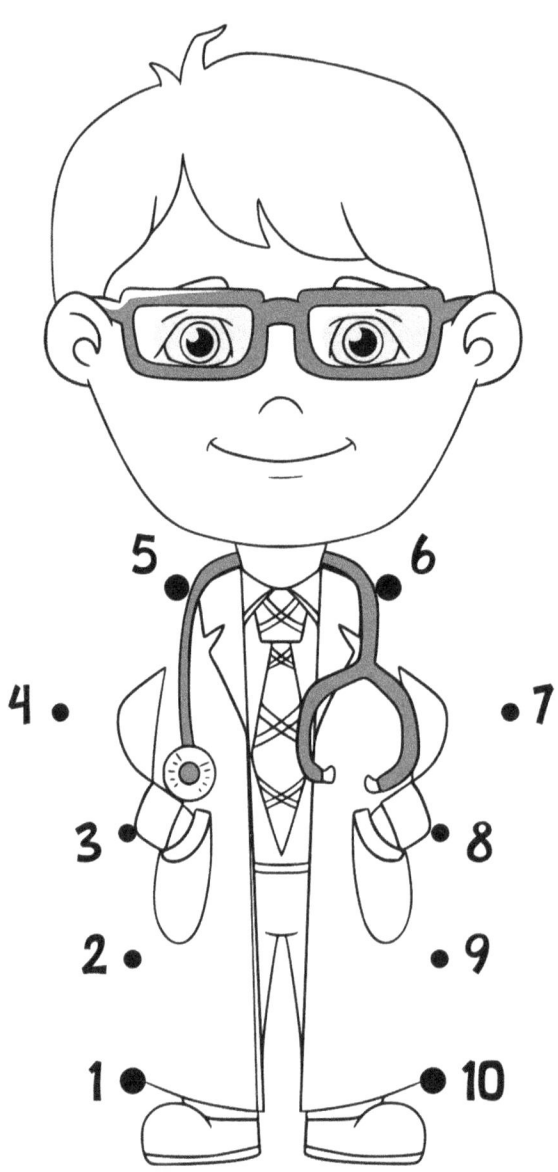

What have you drawn? _____

115

PEOPLE

A garbage man collects our trash.
Circle the 5 differences between the garbage collectors.

PEOPLE

A hospital is where we get treated for different kinds of diseases. Mark an x over the 5 people that shouldn't be in a hospital.

PEOPLE

When there's a fire in your neighborhood, you should call the fire fighters to put out the fire. Draw the other half of the firefighter.

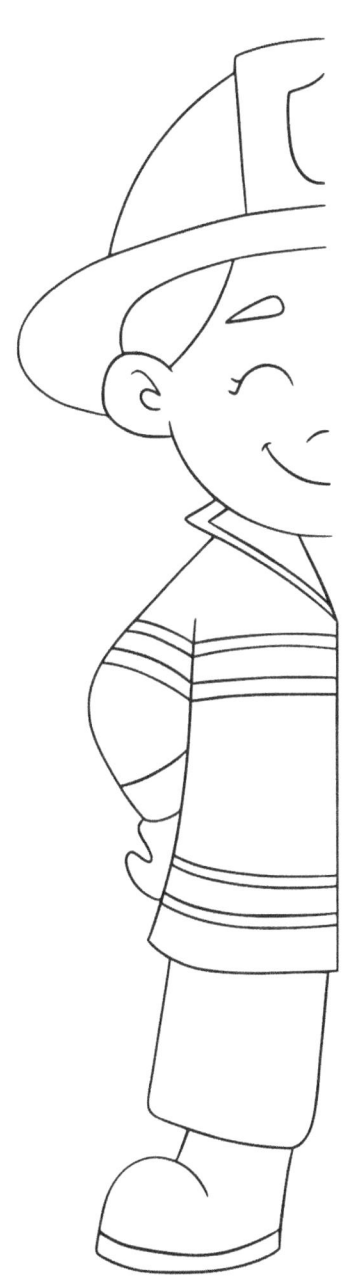

PEOPLE

Draw a line to connect the item on the left to the professional on the right.

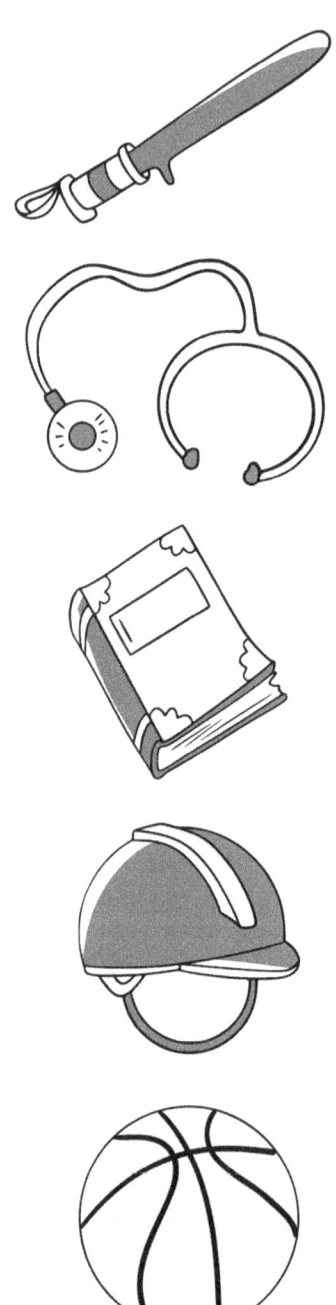

PEOPLE

Find these 5 words in the grid:

POLICE　　DOCTOR　　TEACHER　　FARMER　　LAWYER

P	B	C	F	K	S	B	T	C	V
O	U	L	A	R	H	X	E	N	U
L	D	I	R	X	O	L	A	F	S
I	G	Q	M	H	U	H	C	A	G
C	H	J	E	L	V	C	H	K	S
E	S	Y	R	U	S	Q	E	L	D
B	X	D	O	C	T	O	R	V	N
R	D	X	C	A	R	X	Y	U	O
H	D	V	S	O	C	T	Z	I	V
N	H	G	L	A	W	Y	E	R	U

PEOPLE

The mailman delivers our mail.
Connect the dots and see what you have drawn.

What have you drawn? _____

121

PEOPLE

**Every professional wears a uniform.
Circle the professional in every comparison.**

PEOPLE

The police station is where you can find all police officers. Color the illustration below, according to number.

| 1 | GREEN | 3 | ORANGE | 5 | RED |
| 2 | BLUE | 4 | GRAY | 6 | YELLOW |

PEOPLE

**Doctors and nurses have their own kinds of clothes.
Circle 5 persons in medical clothing.**

PEOPLE

The classroom is where we study as students. Mark an x over the 5 people that shouldn't be in a classroom.

PEOPLE

Circle your answers for each question below.

Who enforces the law and protects the citizens?

Who treats our sickness and illnesses?

Who helps the doctors treat their patients?

Who flies airplanes?

Who fights fires?

VEHICLES

Find these 5 words in the grid:

CAR   BOAT   MOTORCYCLE   AIRPLANE   HELICOPTER

V	H	N	C	K	U	M	U	S	E
S	E	U	L	H	B	O	A	T	A
F	L	G	C	A	O	T	L	E	H
S	I	K	A	R	D	O	A	X	Y
D	C	L	R	D	C	R	C	R	A
V	O	E	X	U	A	C	H	X	H
O	P	R	T	I	O	Y	F	E	S
Z	T	U	W	E	S	C	J	V	Q
Y	E	A	I	R	P	L	A	N	E
V	R	U	Q	O	C	E	D	B	A

VEHICLES

**A motorcycle has 2 wheels.
Connect the dots and see what you have drawn.**

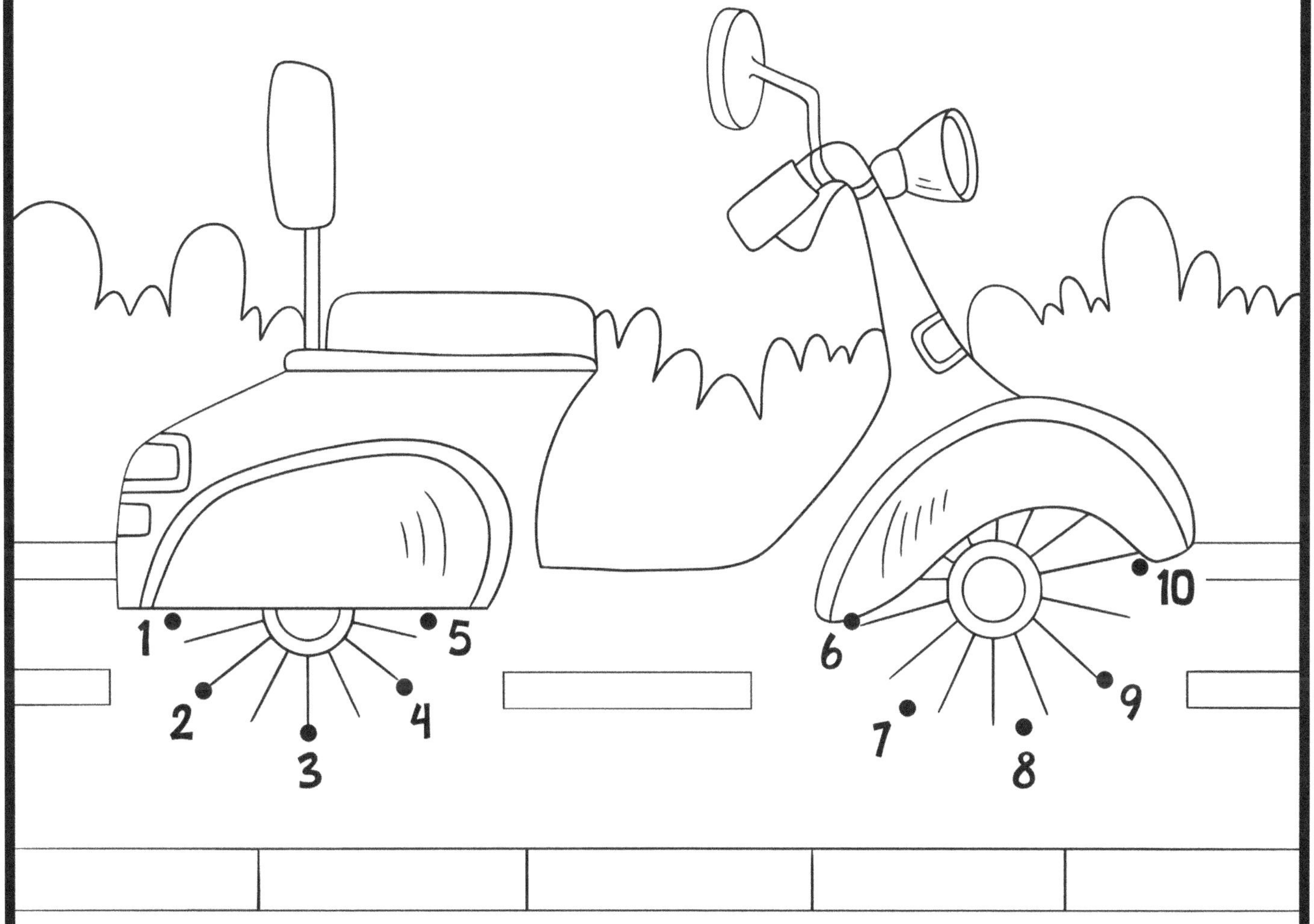

What have you drawn? _____

130

VEHICLES

The police car needs to chase the bandits. Draw a line from the police car to the bandit car, going through the maze.

VEHICLES

Most vehicles have 4 wheels.
Circle 5 vehicles with 4 wheels.

VEHICLES

A cruise ship is a very big ship with lots of people. Connect the dots and see what you have drawn.

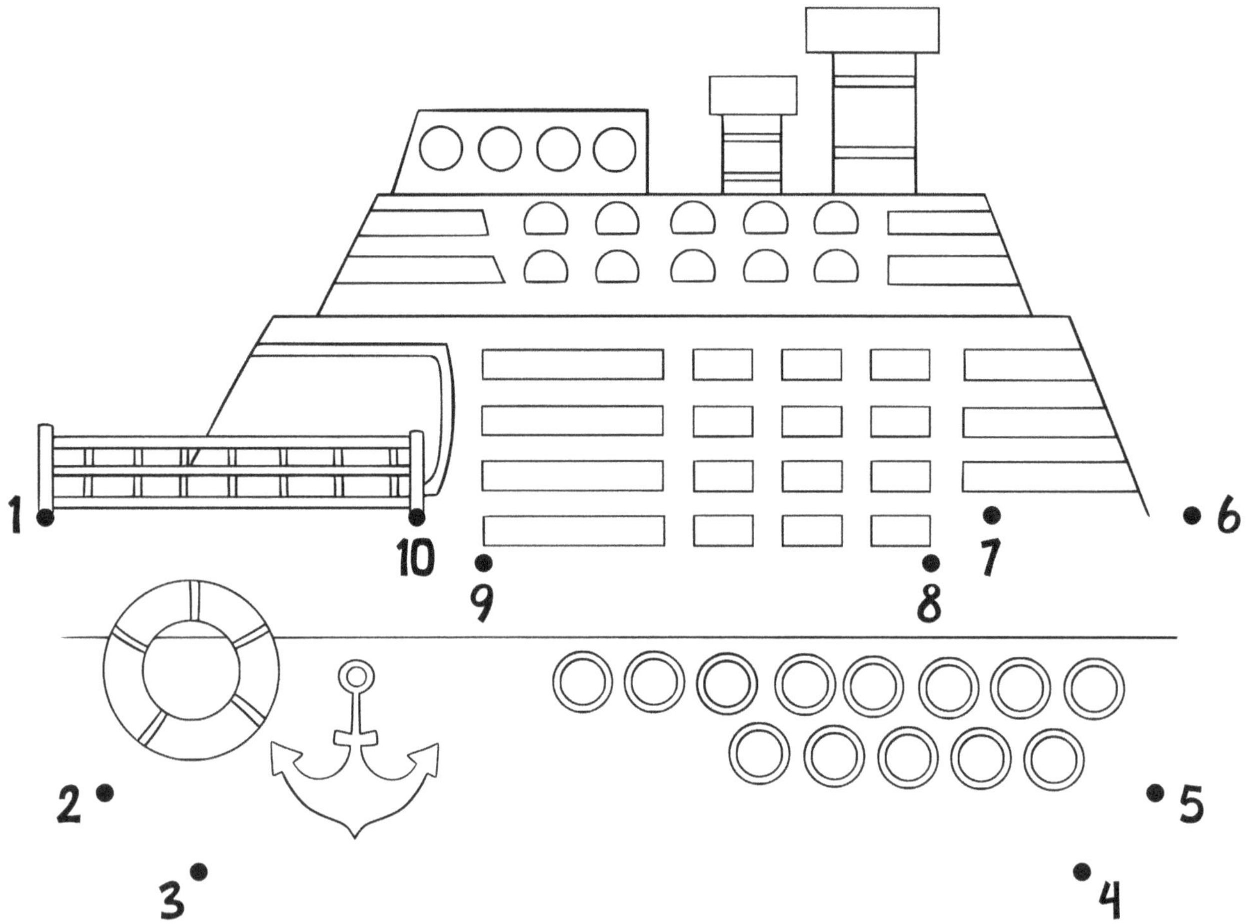

What have you drawn? _____

133

VEHICLES

A bus can bring us from our home to our school. Draw the other half of a school bus.

134

VEHICLES

Draw a line to connect the item on the left to the vehicle on the right.

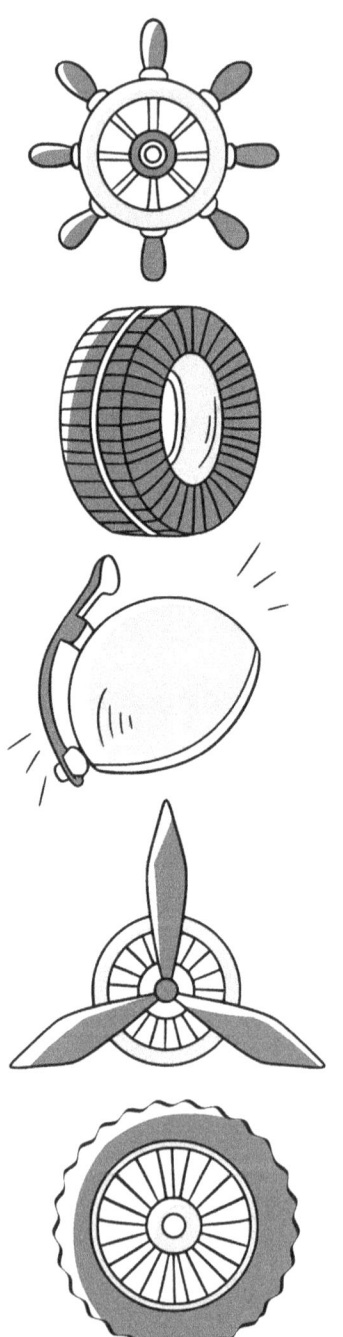

VEHICLES

Boats can float on water.
Mark an x over the 5 vehicles that will not float on water.

136

VEHICLES

A parking lot is where you can park and leave your car. Color the illustration below, according to number.

| 1 | GRAY | 3 | YELLOW | 5 | RED |
| 2 | GREEN | 4 | DARK GREEN | 6 | BLUE |

VEHICLES

A bus stop is where you wait for the bus to arrive. Circle the 5 differences between the bus stops.

138

VEHICLES

A train station is where you wait for the train to arrive. Circle the 5 differences between the train stations.

VEHICLES

A train can transport us from one part of the city to another. Color the illustration below, according to number.

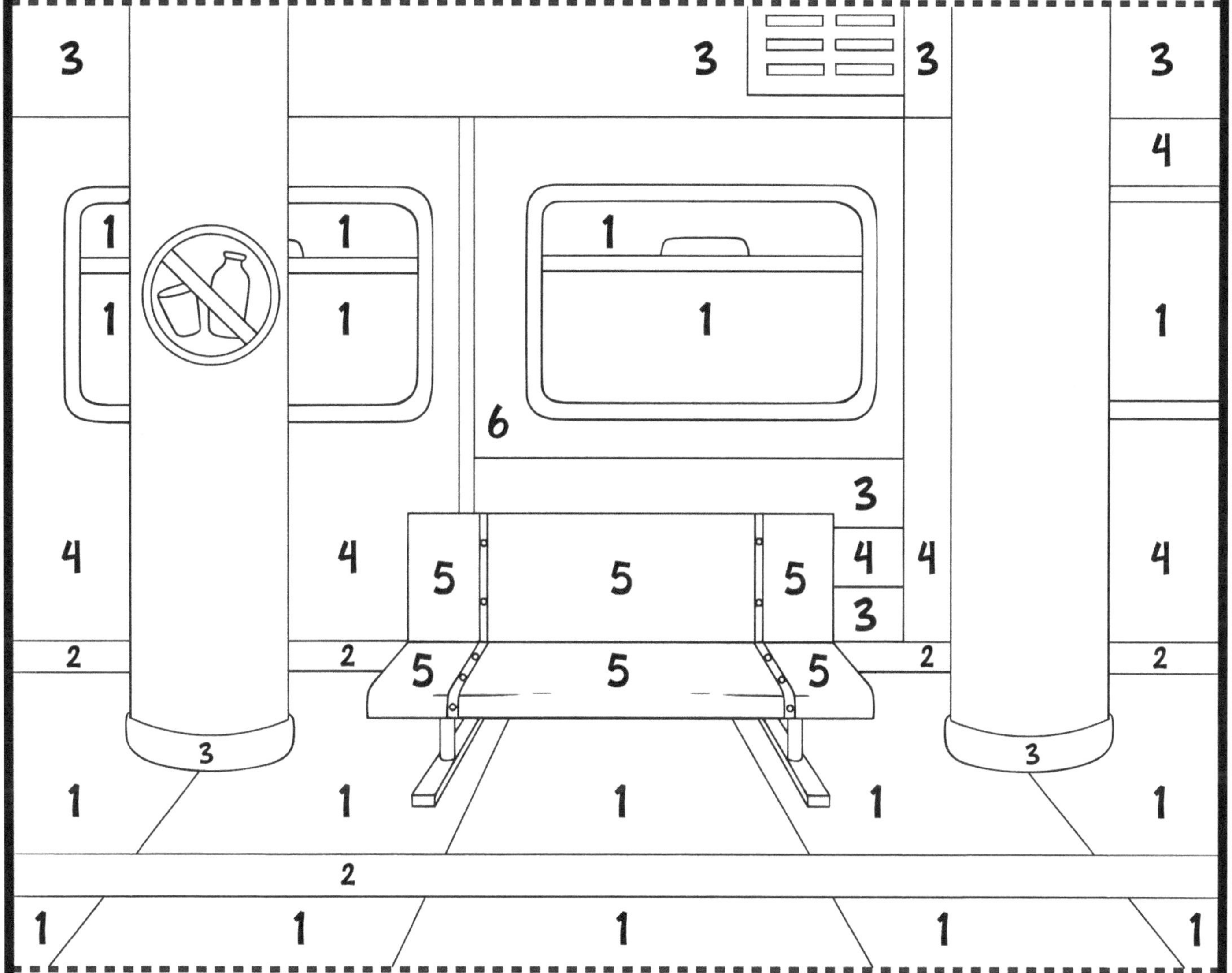

| 1 | GRAY | 3 | PURPLE | 5 | BROWN |
| 2 | YELLOW | 4 | BLUE | 6 | GREEN |

140

VEHICLES

An airport is where you can find airplanes to ride. Mark an x over the 5 vehicles that will not fly.

VEHICLES

Boats can float on water.
Circle 5 vehicles that can float on water.

142

VEHICLES

**Wheels allow vehicles to travel on land.
Circle the wheeled vehicle in every comparison.**

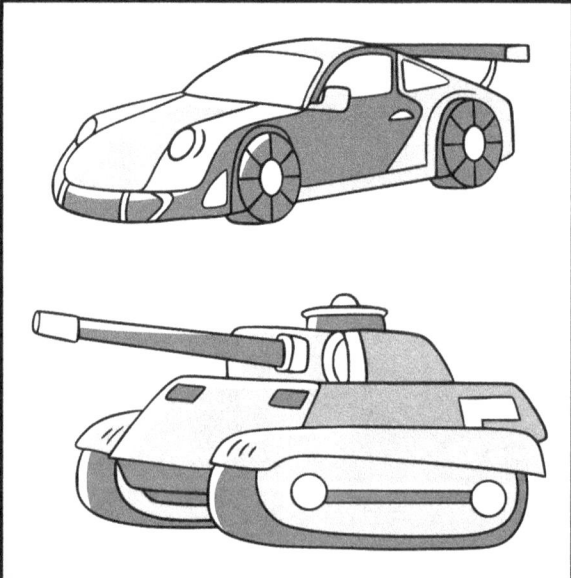

VEHICLES

Circle your answers for each question below.

What has a lot of wheels and transports many people on the road?

What runs on a track and has many cars?

  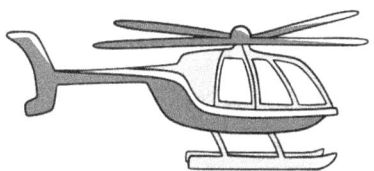

What floats on water?

What collects garbage from the garbage bins?

What can flight high in the sky?

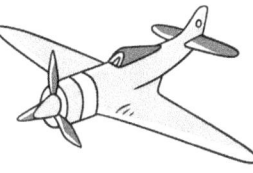  

ANSWER KEY

3 PLACES

4 PLACES

5 PLACES

Differences :

6 PLACES

7 PLACES

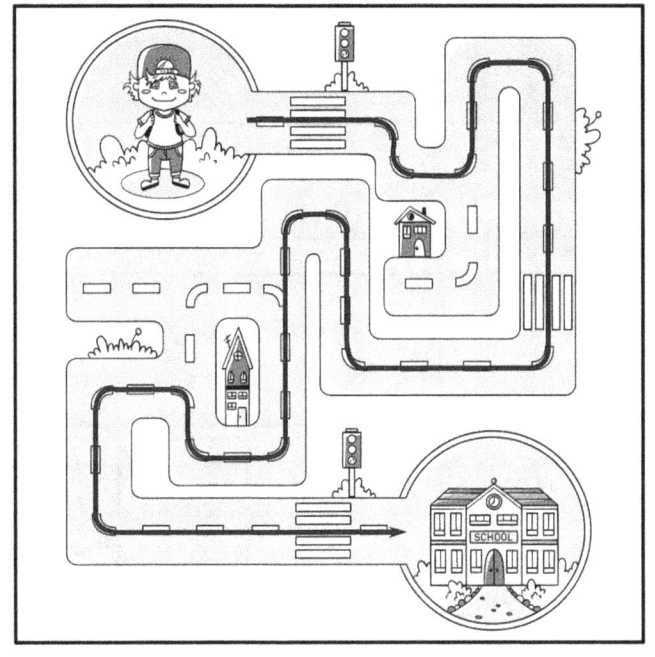

8 PLACES

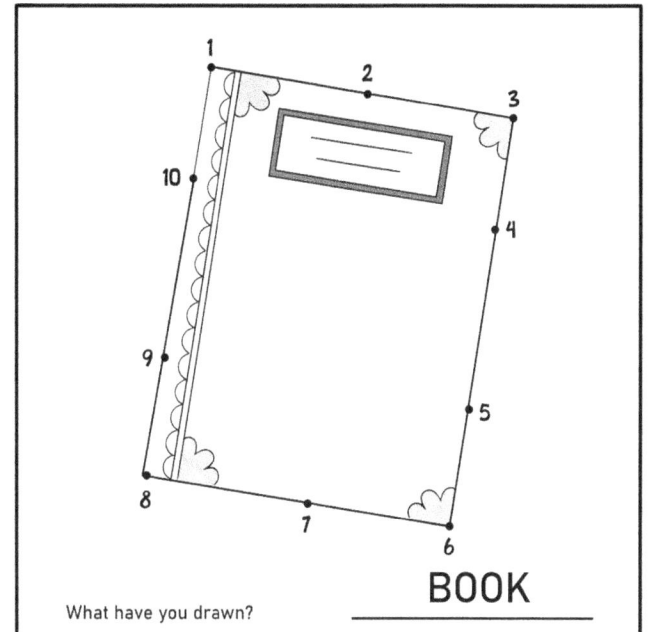

What have you drawn? _____BOOK_____

9 PLACES

10 PLACES

148

11 PLACES

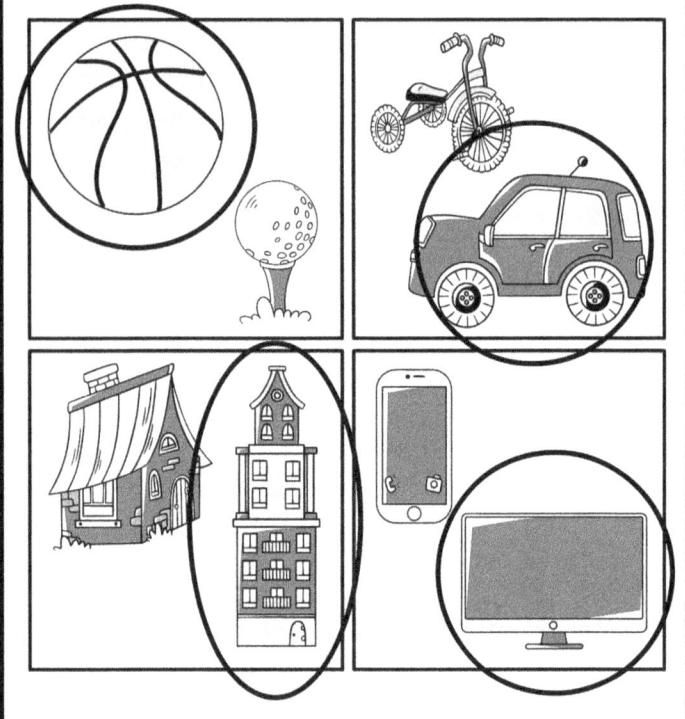

12 PLACES

Which one has more people?

Which one has taller buildings?

Which one has less people?

13 PLACES

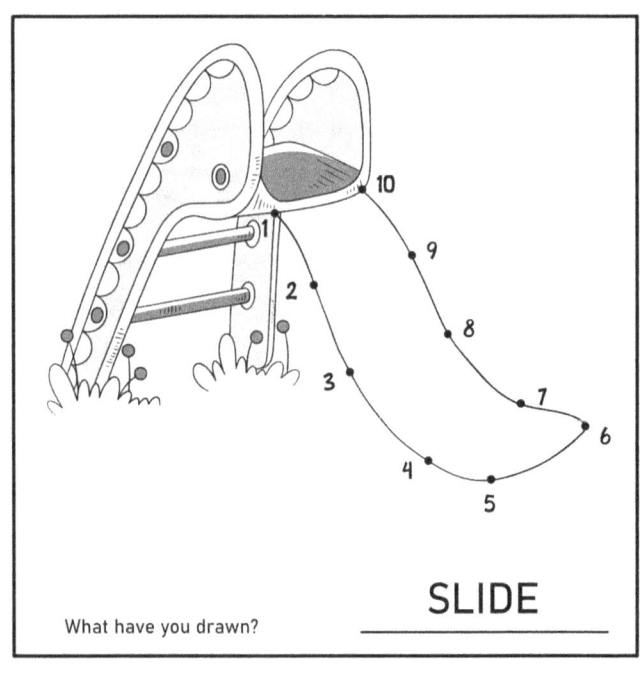

What have you drawn? SLIDE

149

14 PLACES

Differences :

15 PLACES

16 PLACES

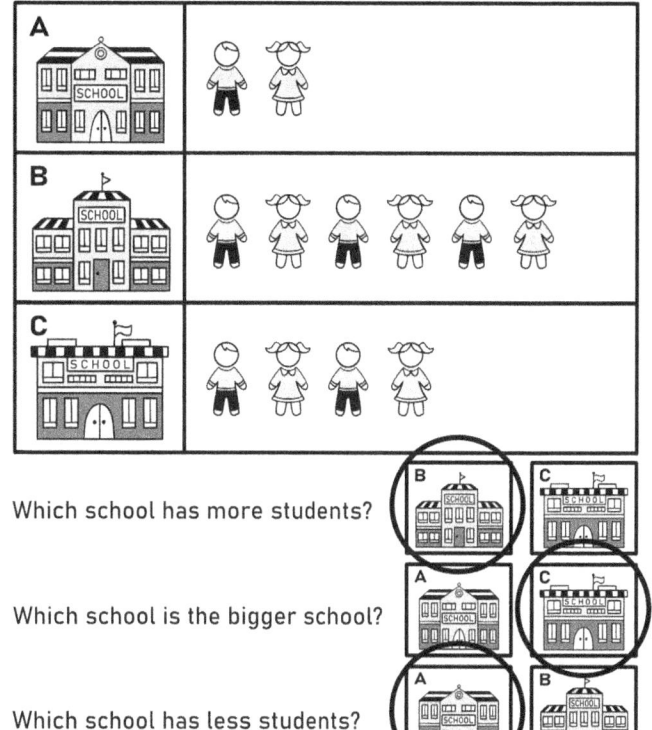

Which school has more students?

Which school is the bigger school?

Which school has less students?

17 PLACES

18 PLACES

Where do students study?

Where do you find a collection of a lot of books that you can borrow?

Library / House / Office

Where can you spend your day playing with friends?

Office / Library / Playground

Which place has more people?

Farm / Town / City

Where can you find a fire truck?

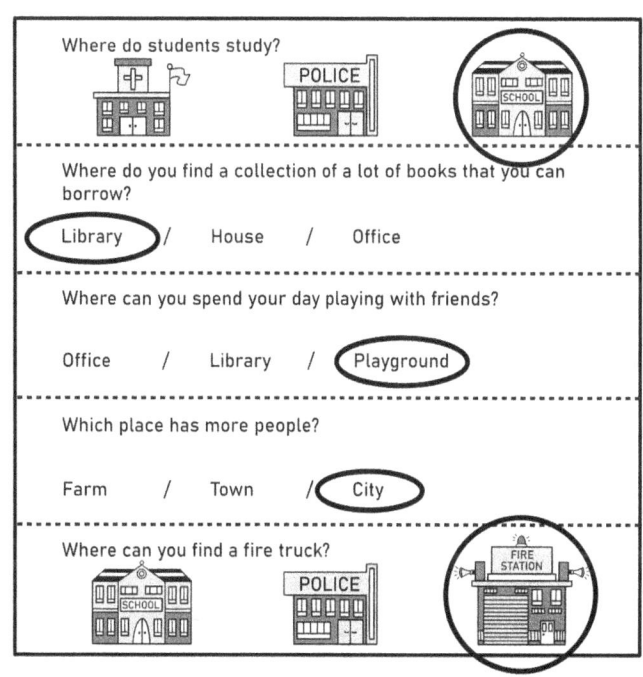

21 NATURE

22 NATURE

23 NATURE

Differences :

151

24 NATURE

V	Q	E	L	G	R	H
O	K	N	W	V	T	I
L	O	C	E	A	N	L
C	U	F	Y	D	S	L
A	R	O	C	K	S	Z
N	I	P	O	X	H	J
O	M	R	I	V	E	R

25 NATURE

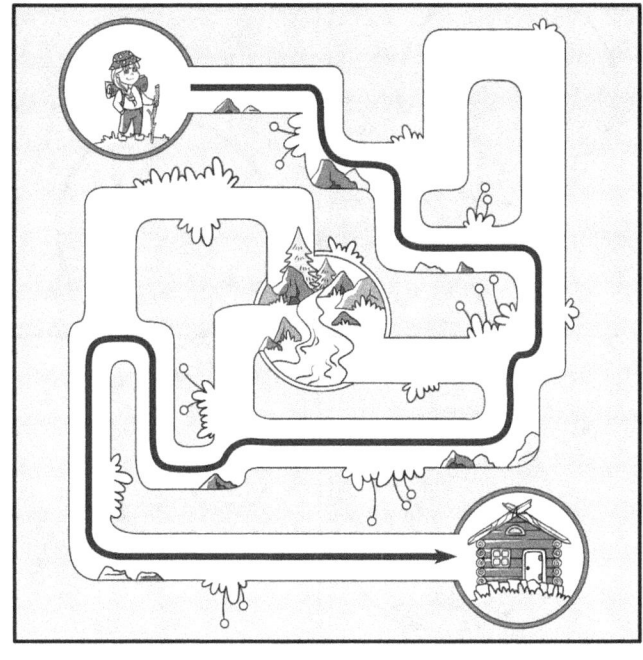

26 NATURE

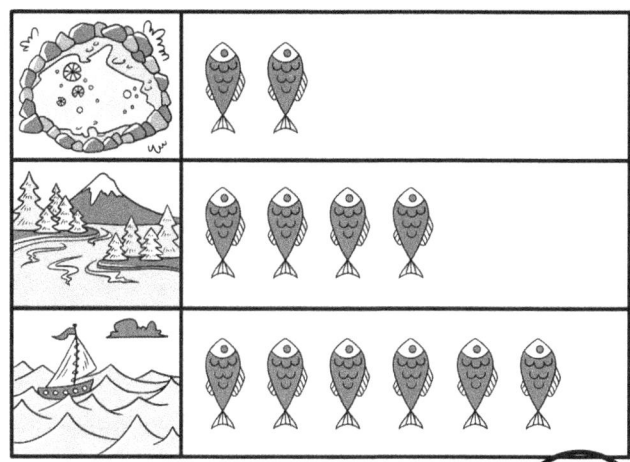

Which one has more fish?

Which one has more water?

The ocean has more fish than the pond. (TRUE) / FALSE

27 NATURE

28 NATURE

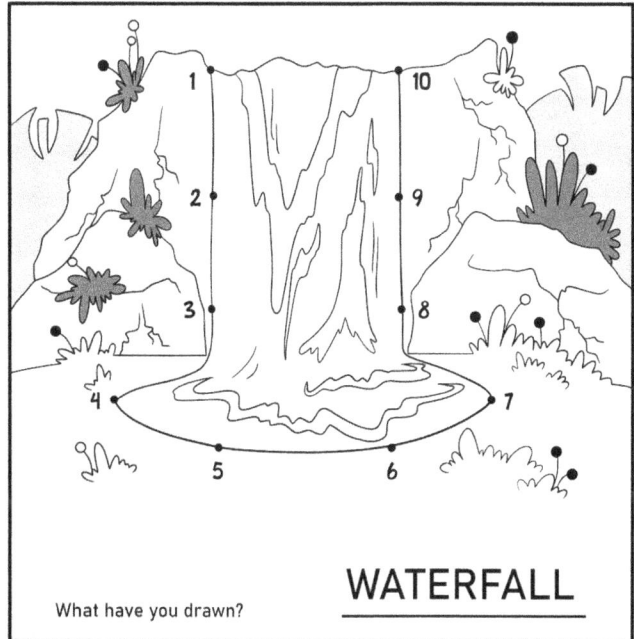

What have you drawn? __WATERFALL__

152

29 NATURE

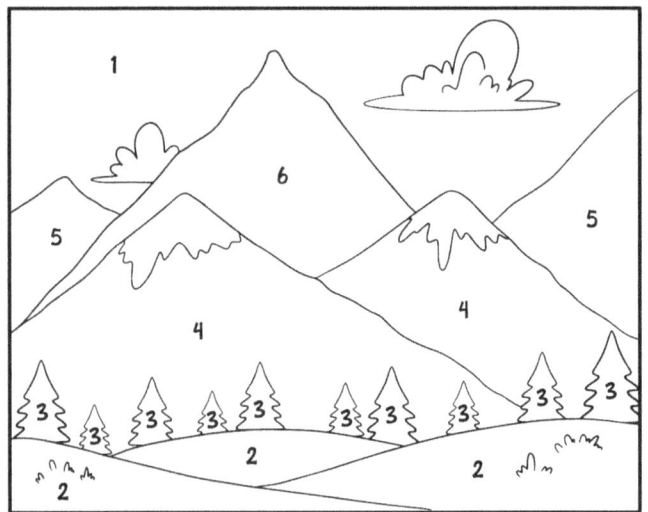

30 NATURE

31 NATURE

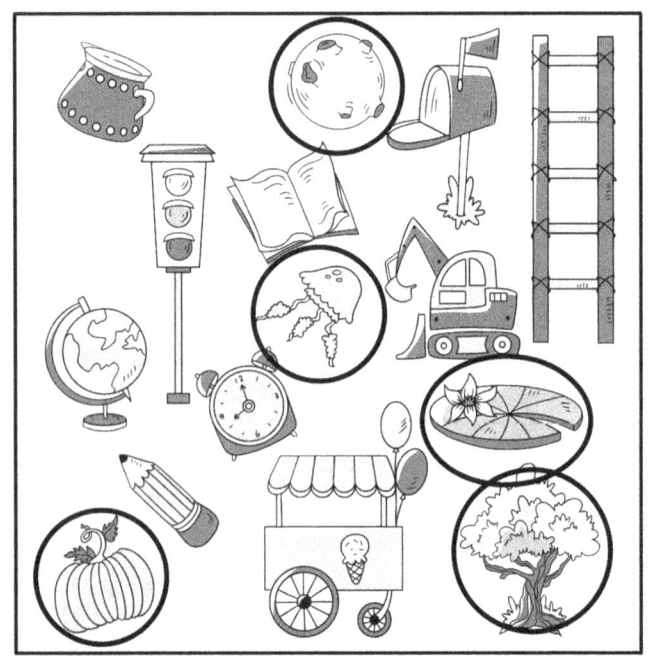

32 NATURE

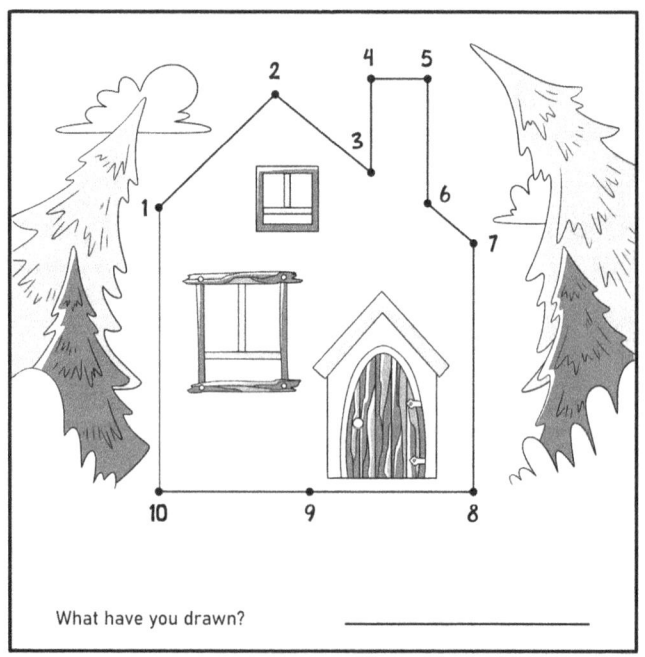

What have you drawn? _____

33 NATURE

Differences:

34 NATURE

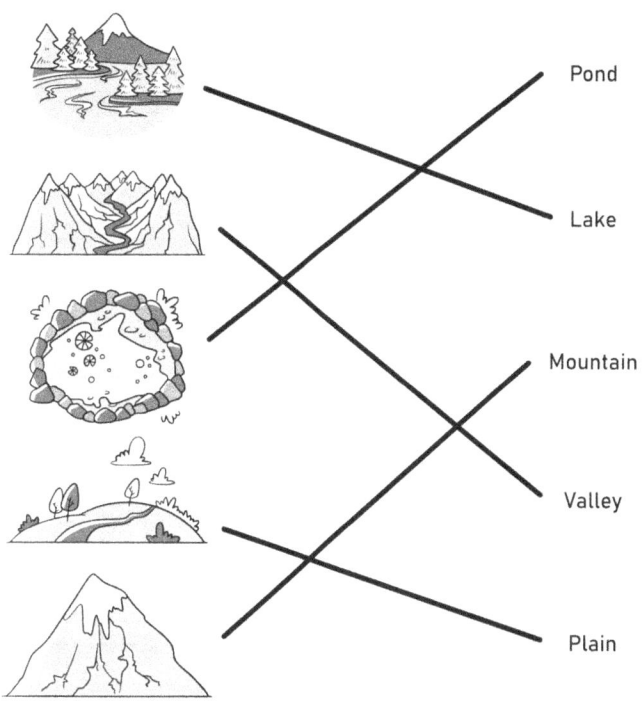

Pond
Lake
Mountain
Valley
Plain

35 NATURE

36 NATURE

Which one is the largest body of water?

Pond / Lake / (Ocean)

Where can you find a lot of tall trees?

(Forest) / Desert / Grassland

Which one spews out hot magma when it erupts?

Where can you find sharks and whales?

(Ocean) / River / Savannah

Which one has flowing water?

Lake / (River) / Valley

154

39 WEATHER

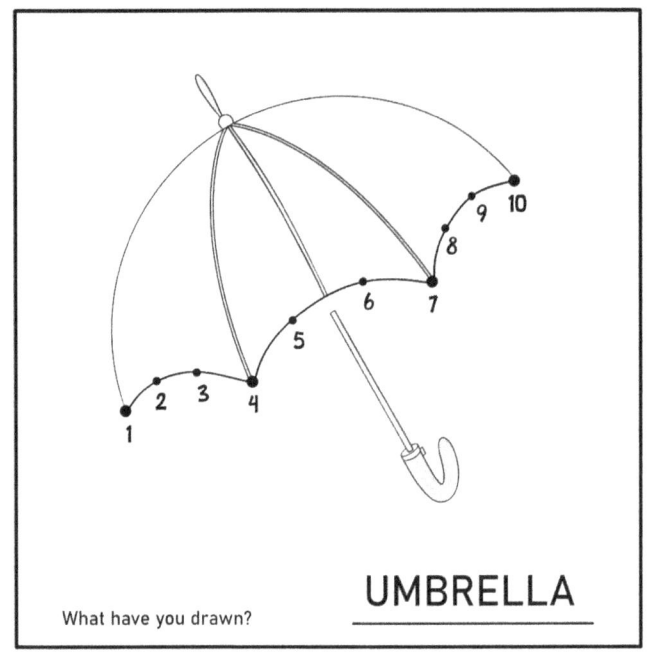

What have you drawn? UMBRELLA

40 WEATHER

41 WEATHER

42 WEATHER

43 WEATHER

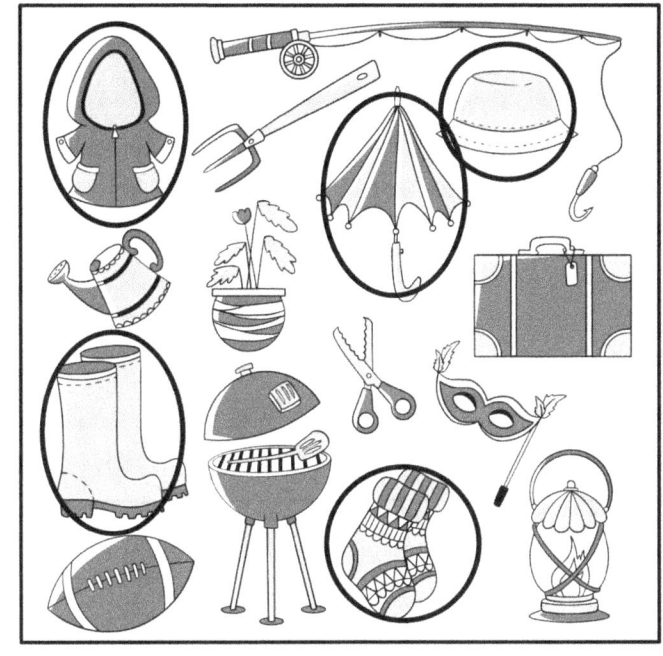

44 WEATHER

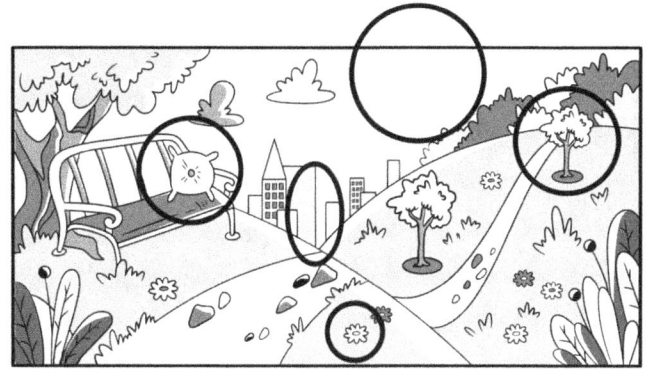

45 WEATHER

46 WEATHER

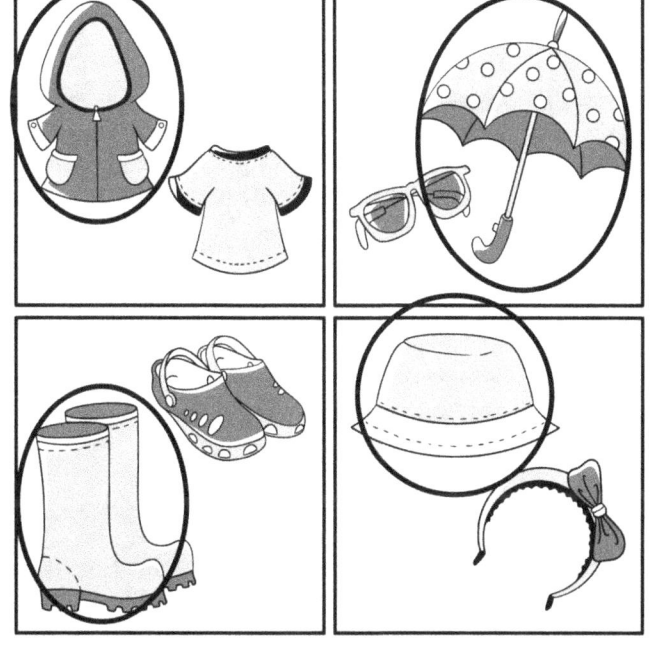

47 WEATHER

What have you drawn? SNOWMAN

48 WEATHER

49 WEATHER

50 WEATHER

157

51 WEATHER

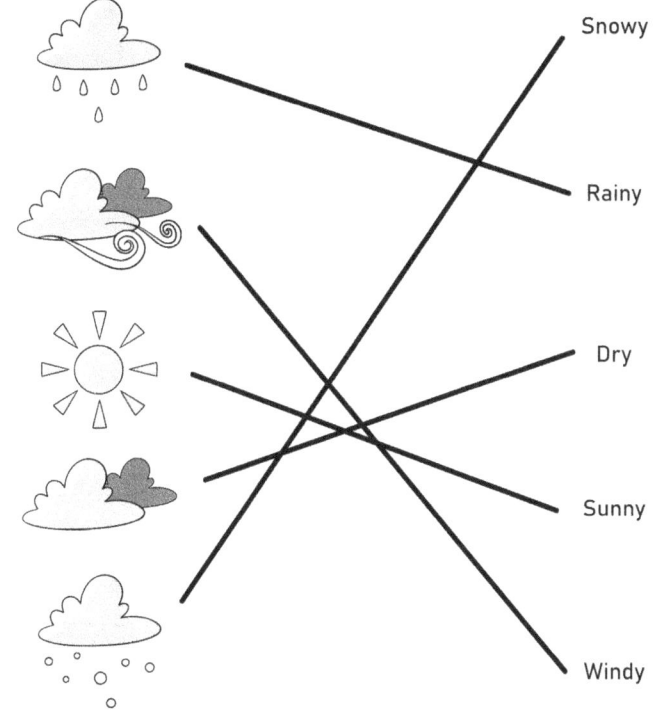

52 WEATHER

53 WEATHER

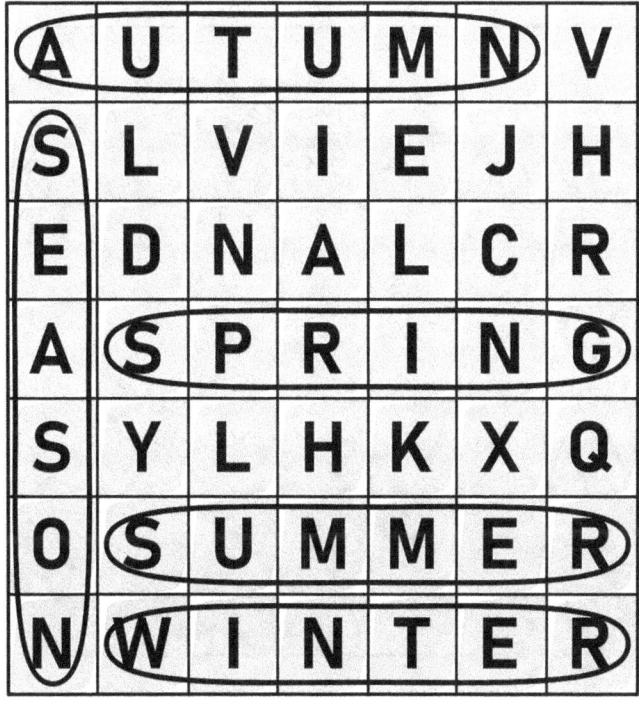

54 WEATHER

Which one is part of the four seasons?

Rainy / (Winter) / Windy

When can you use a raincoat?

(Rainy) / Sunny / Snowy

Which symbol stands for sunny?

Which one can you build in the snow?

When can you fly a kite?

(Windy) / Sunny / Raining

158

57 PLANTS

U	R	O	C	K	L	D	M
C	O	C	O	N	U	T	R
M	V	J	H	W	P	R	B
A	N	X	R	T	S	E	A
N	Q	I	N	E	D	E	U
G	H	A	C	O	R	N	H
O	R	M	Y	E	V	U	G
M	B	A	J	R	B	Q	E

58 PLANTS

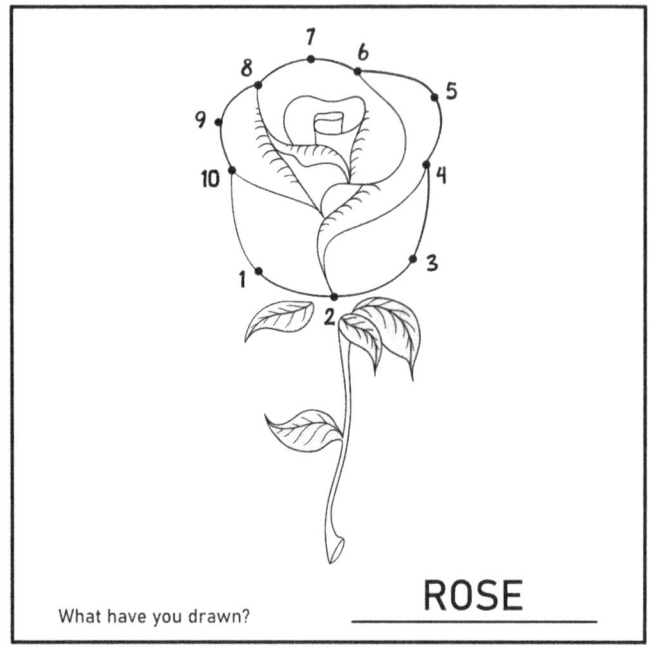

What have you drawn? _____ROSE_____

59 PLANTS

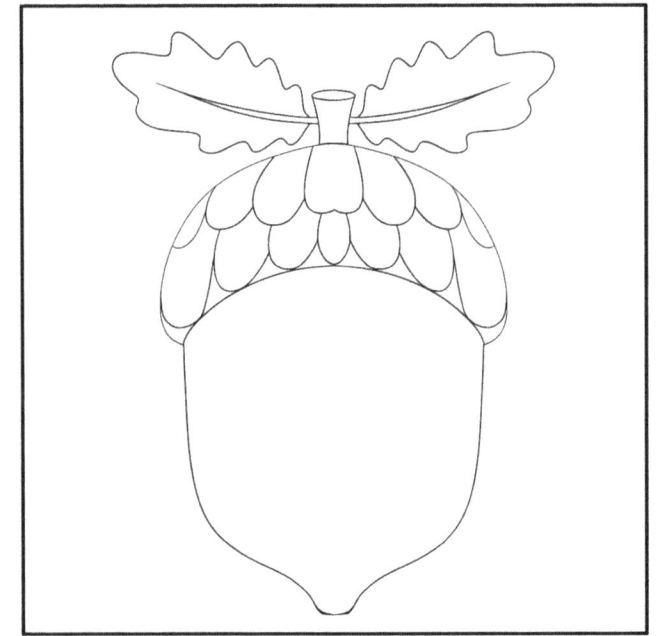

159

60 PLANTS

61 PLANTS

62 PLANTS

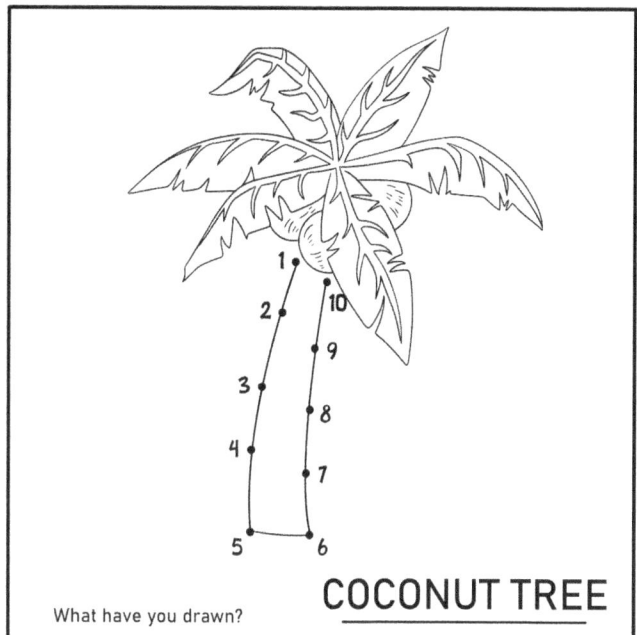

What have you drawn? **COCONUT TREE**

63 PLANTS

64 PLANTS

65 PLANTS

Differences :

66 PLANTS

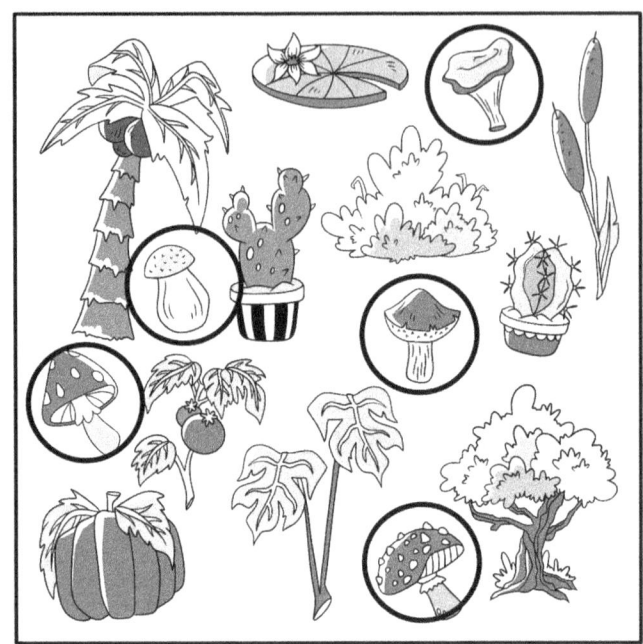

67 PLANTS

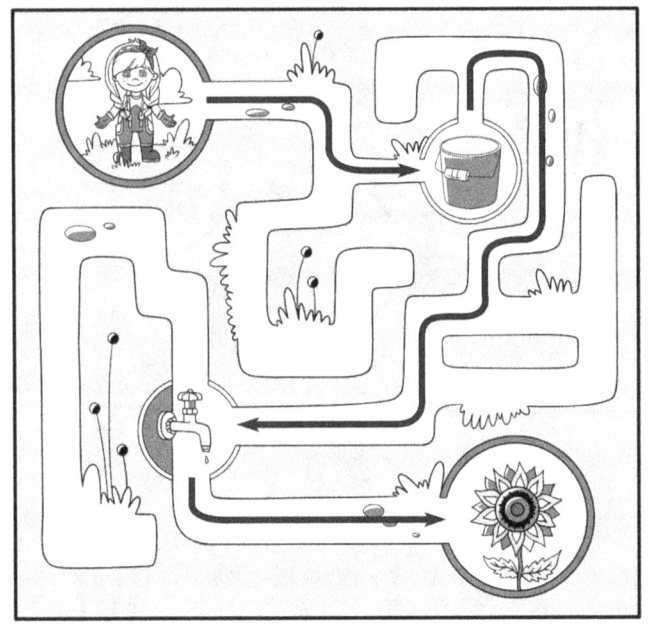

161

68 PLANTS

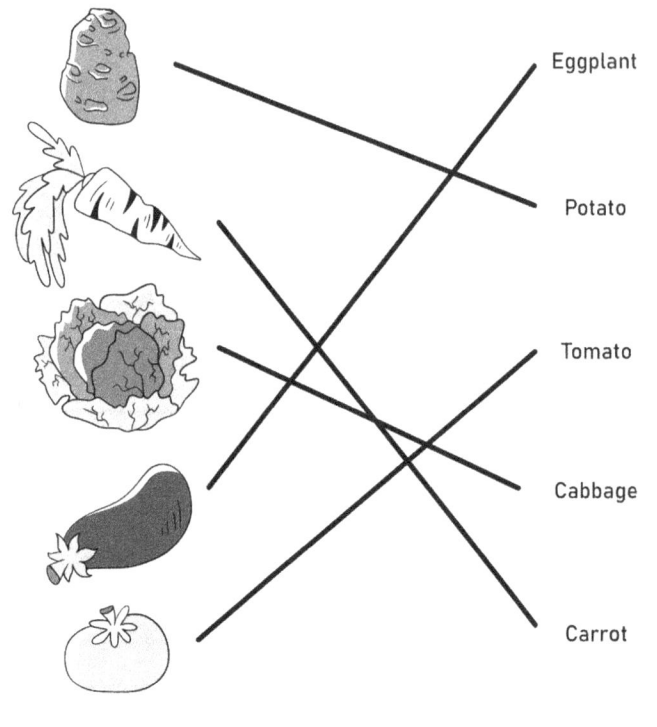

Eggplant

Potato

Tomato

Cabbage

Carrot

69 PLANTS

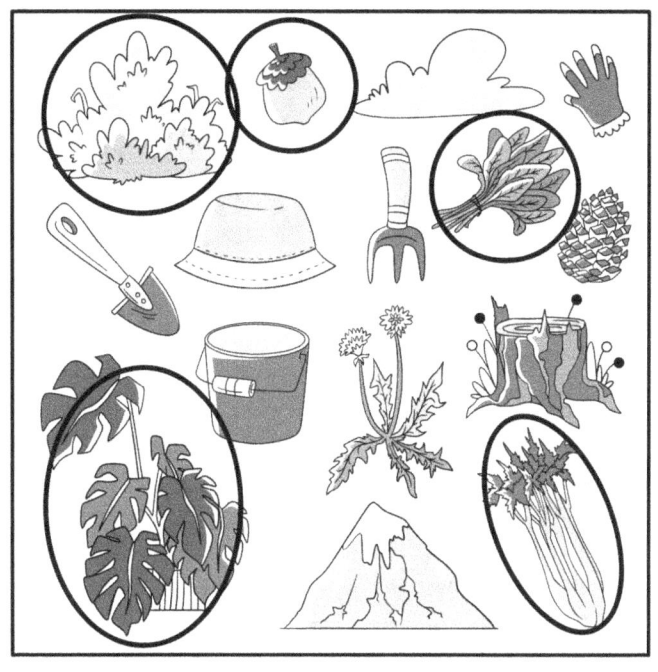

70 PLANTS

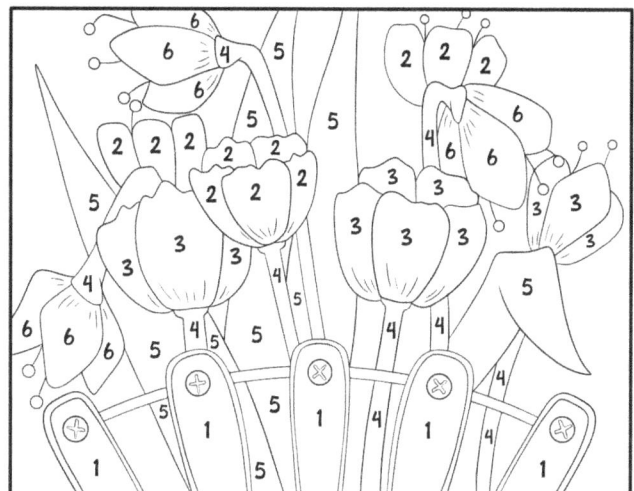

71 PLANTS

Differences :

72 PLANTS

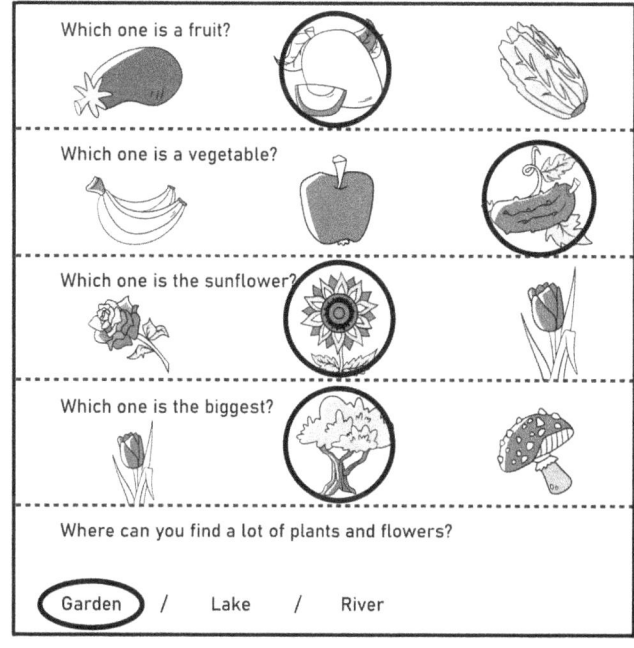

75 ANIMALS

76 ANIMALS

G	I	R	A	F	F	E	B
V	D	K	N	Q	H	C	S
L	W	J	L	K	O	L	X
I	Z	U	S	C	R	D	C
O	Y	V	O	X	S	Q	B
N	I	C	M	B	E	A	R
X	V	O	R	O	L	C	D
E	L	E	P	H	A	N	T

77 ANIMALS

Differences :

78 ANIMALS

163

79 ANIMALS

80 ANIMALS

81 ANIMALS

Differences :

82 ANIMALS

83 ANIMALS

84 ANIMALS
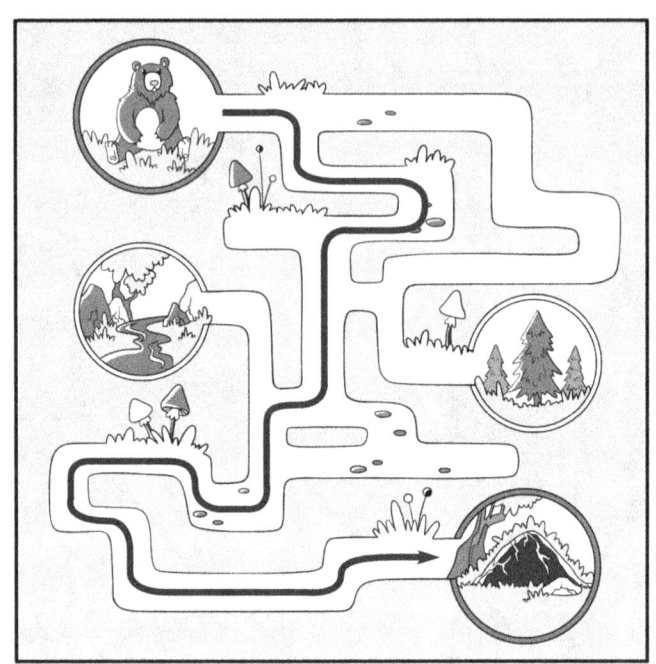

85 ANIMALS
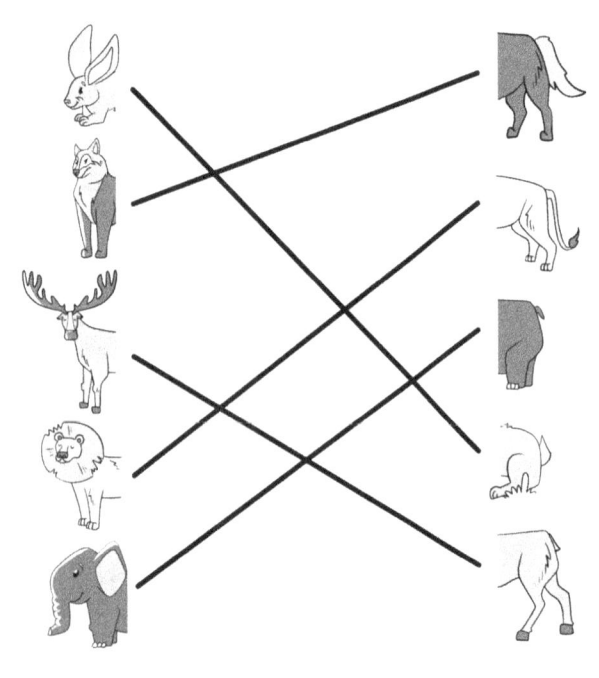

86 ANIMALS
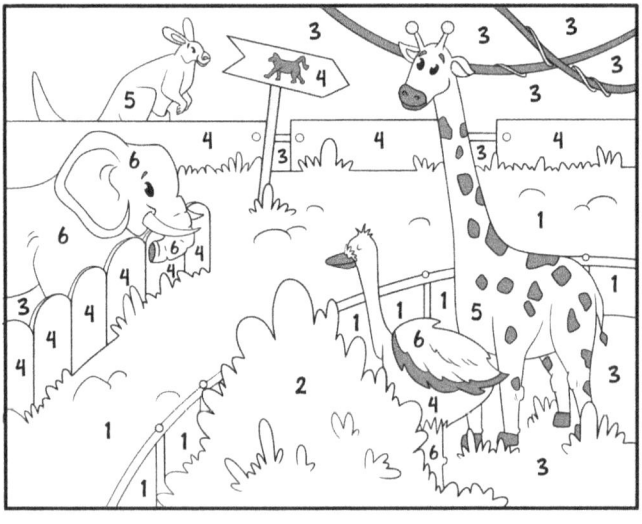

165

87 ANIMALS

What have you drawn? __RABBIT__

88 ANIMALS

89 ANIMALS

What have you drawn? __PIG__

90 ANIMALS

166

93 FOOD

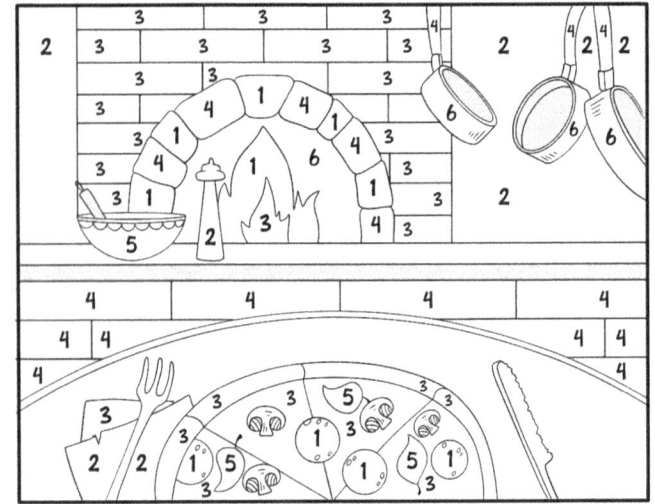

94 FOOD

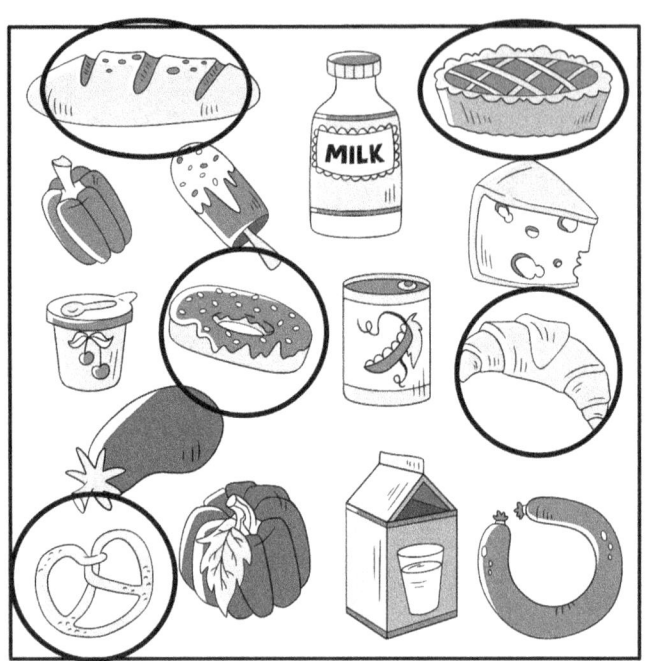

95 FOOD

Differences:

96 FOOD

97 FOOD

98 FOOD

99 FOOD

Differences :

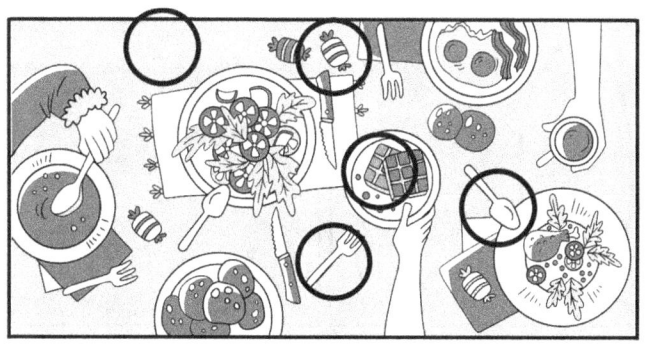

100 FOOD

101 FOOD

102 FOOD
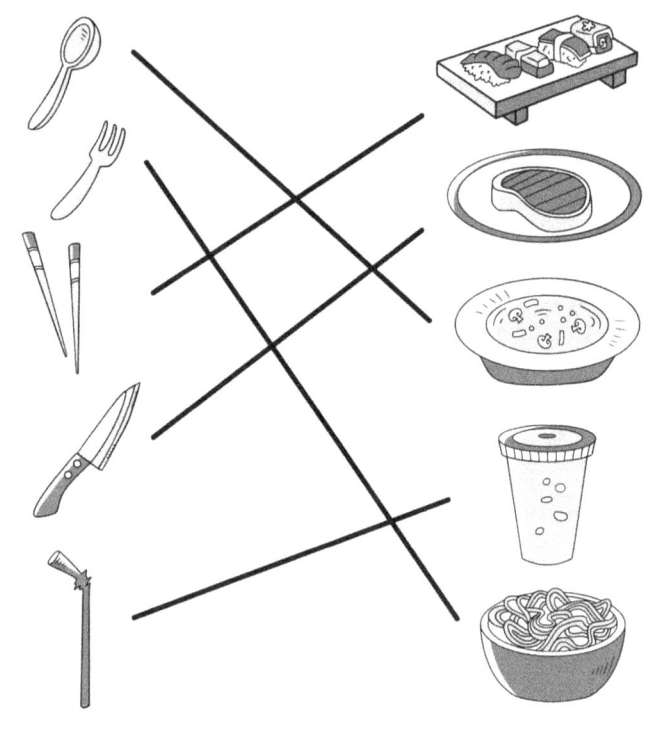

103 FOOD
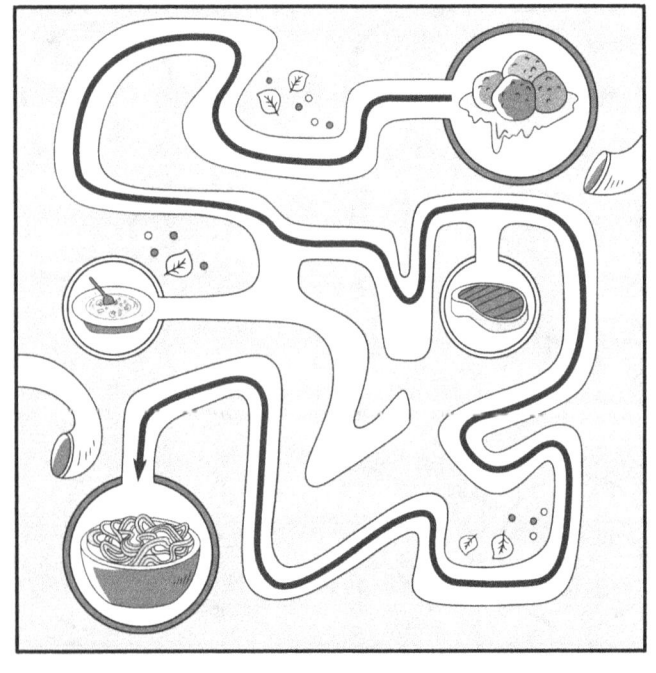

169

104 FOOD
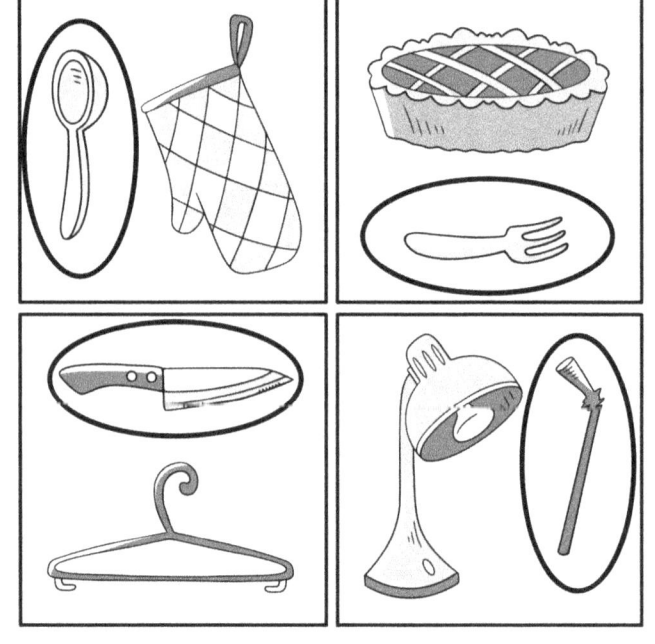

105 FOOD

What have you drawn? **COOKING POT**

106 FOOD

107 FOOD

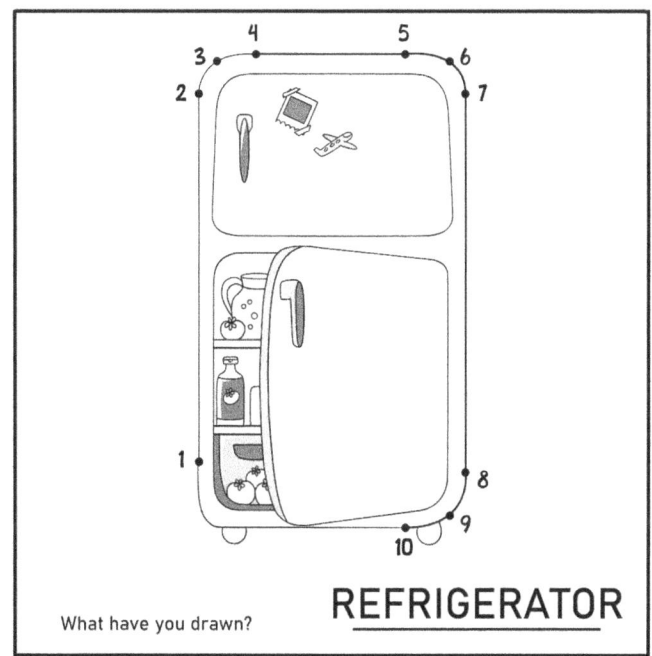

What have you drawn? **REFRIGERATOR**

108 FOOD

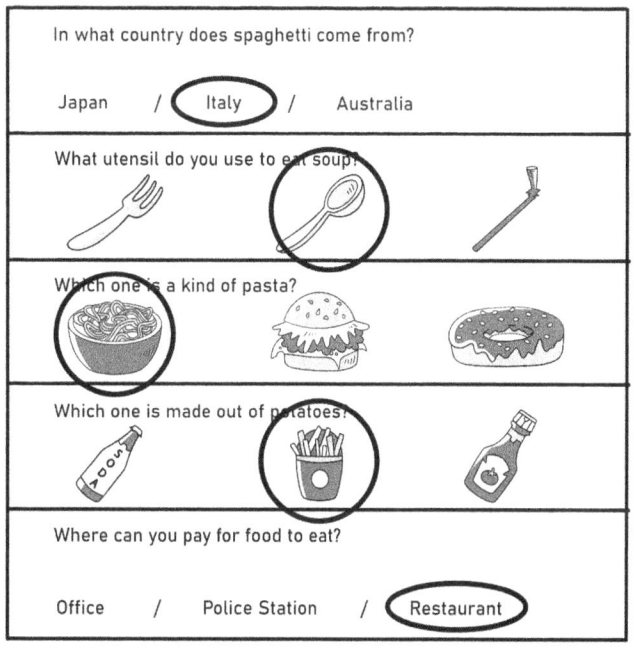

111 PEOPLE

Differences:

112 PEOPLE

113 PEOPLE

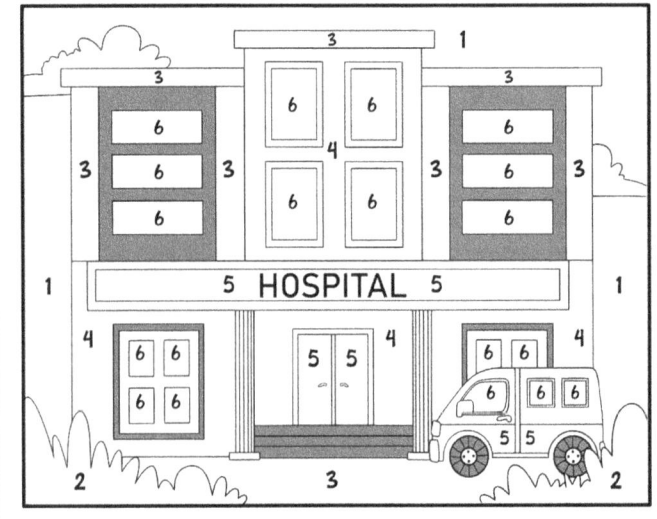

171

114 PEOPLE

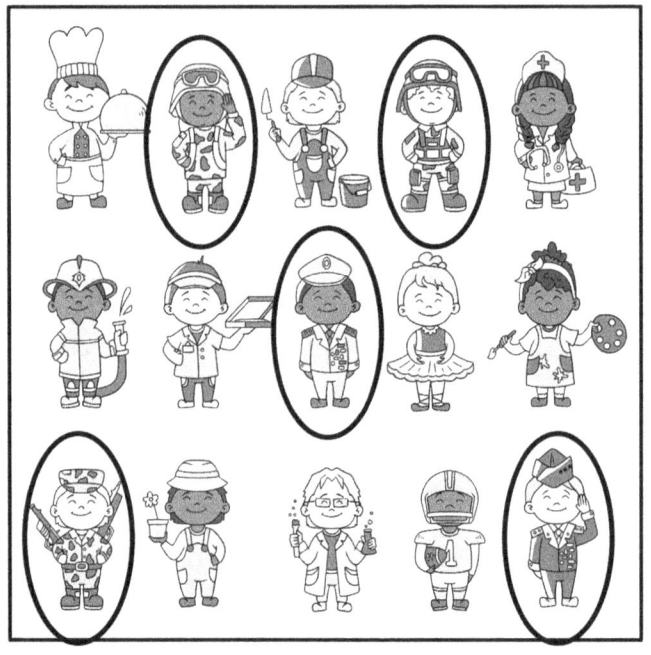

115 PEOPLE

What have you drawn? __DOCTOR__

116 PEOPLE

Differences :

117 PEOPLE

118 PEOPLE

119 PEOPLE

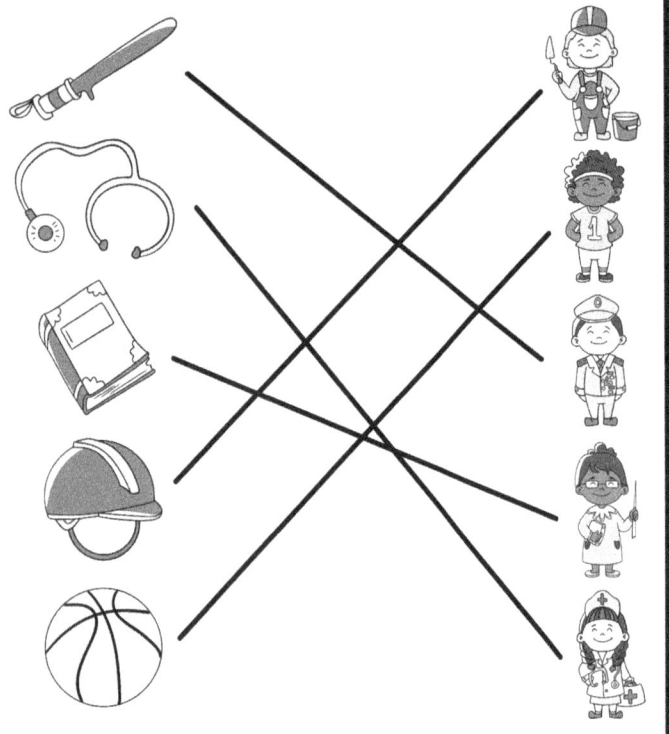

120 PEOPLE

P	B	C	F	K	S	B	I	C	V
O	U	L	A	R	H	X	E	N	U
L	D	I	R	X	O	L	A	F	S
I	G	Q	M	H	U	H	C	A	G
C	H	J	E	L	V	C	H	K	S
E	S	Y	R	U	S	Q	E	L	D
B	X	D	O	C	T	O	R	V	N
R	D	X	C	A	R	X	Y	U	O
H	D	V	S	O	C	T	Z	I	V
N	H	G	L	A	W	Y	E	R	U

121 PEOPLE

What have you drawn? _____MAILMAN_____

173

122 PEOPLE

123 PEOPLE

124 PEOPLE

125 PEOPLE

126 PEOPLE

129 VEHICLES

V	A	N	C	K	U	M	U	S	E
S	E	U	L	H	B	O	A	T	A
F	L	G	C	A	O	T	L	E	H
S	I	K	A	R	D	O	A	X	Y
D	C	L	R	D	C	R	C	R	A
V	O	E	X	U	A	C	H	X	H
O	P	R	T	I	O	Y	F	E	S
Z	T	U	W	E	S	C	J	V	Q
Y	E	A	I	R	P	L	A	N	E
V	R	U	Q	O	C	E	D	B	A

130 VEHICLES

What have you drawn?   MOTORCYCLE

131 VEHICLES

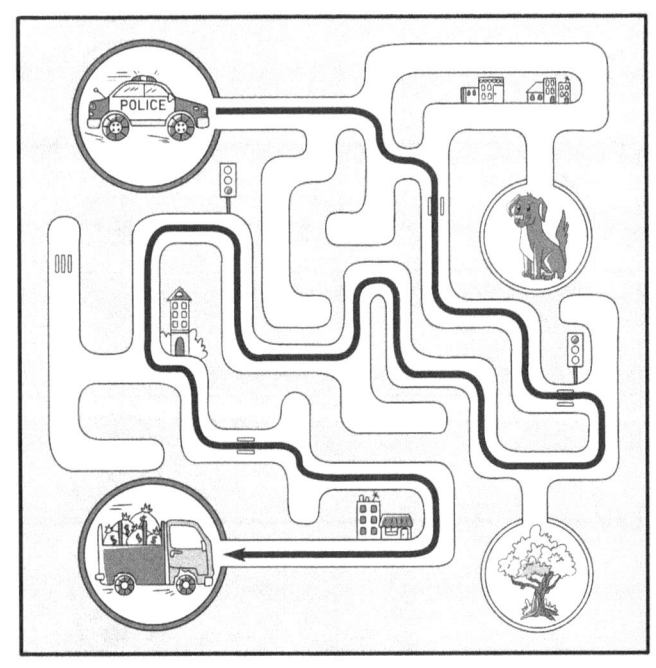

132 VEHICLES

133 VEHICLES

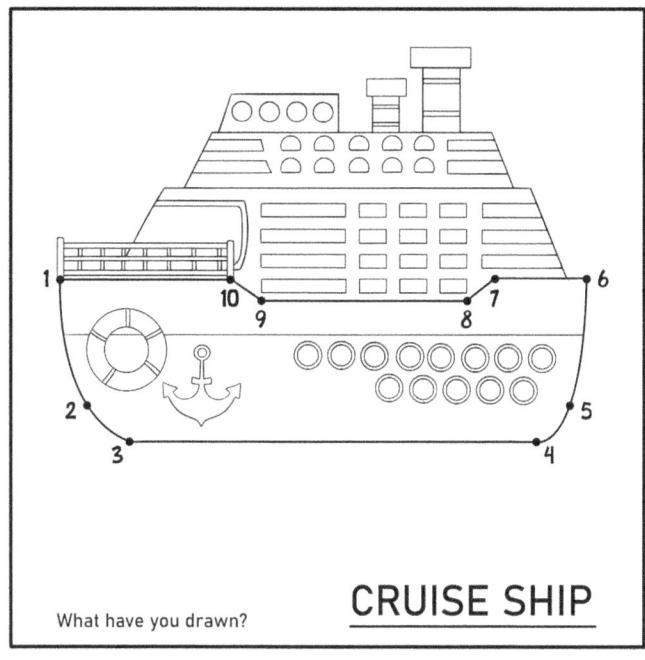

What have you drawn? CRUISE SHIP

134 VEHICLES

135 VEHICLES

136 VEHICLES

176

137 VEHICLES

138 VEHICLES

Differences :

139 VEHICLES

Differences :

140 VEHICLES

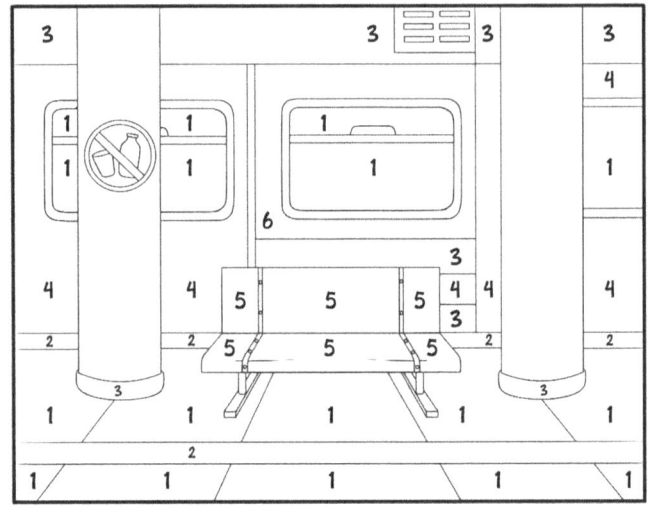

141 VEHICLES

142 VEHICLES

143 VEHICLES

144 VEHICLES

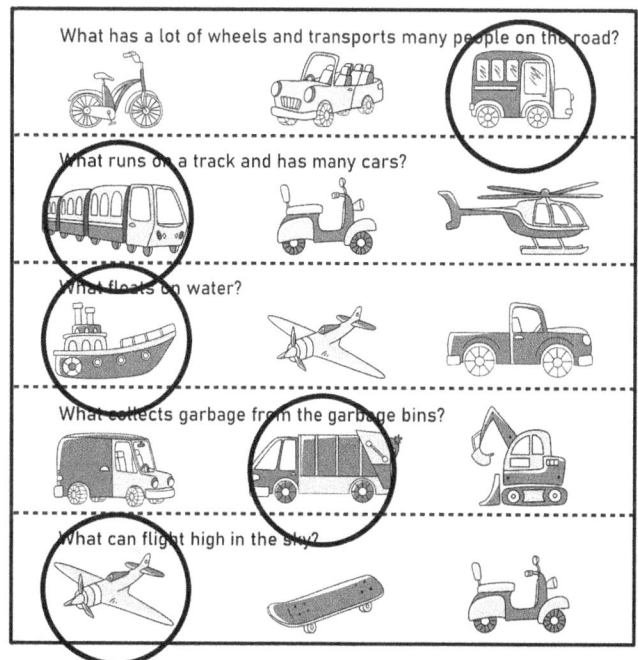

What has a lot of wheels and transports many people on the road?

What runs on a track and has many cars?

What floats on water?

What collects garbage from the garbage bins?

What can flight high in the sky?

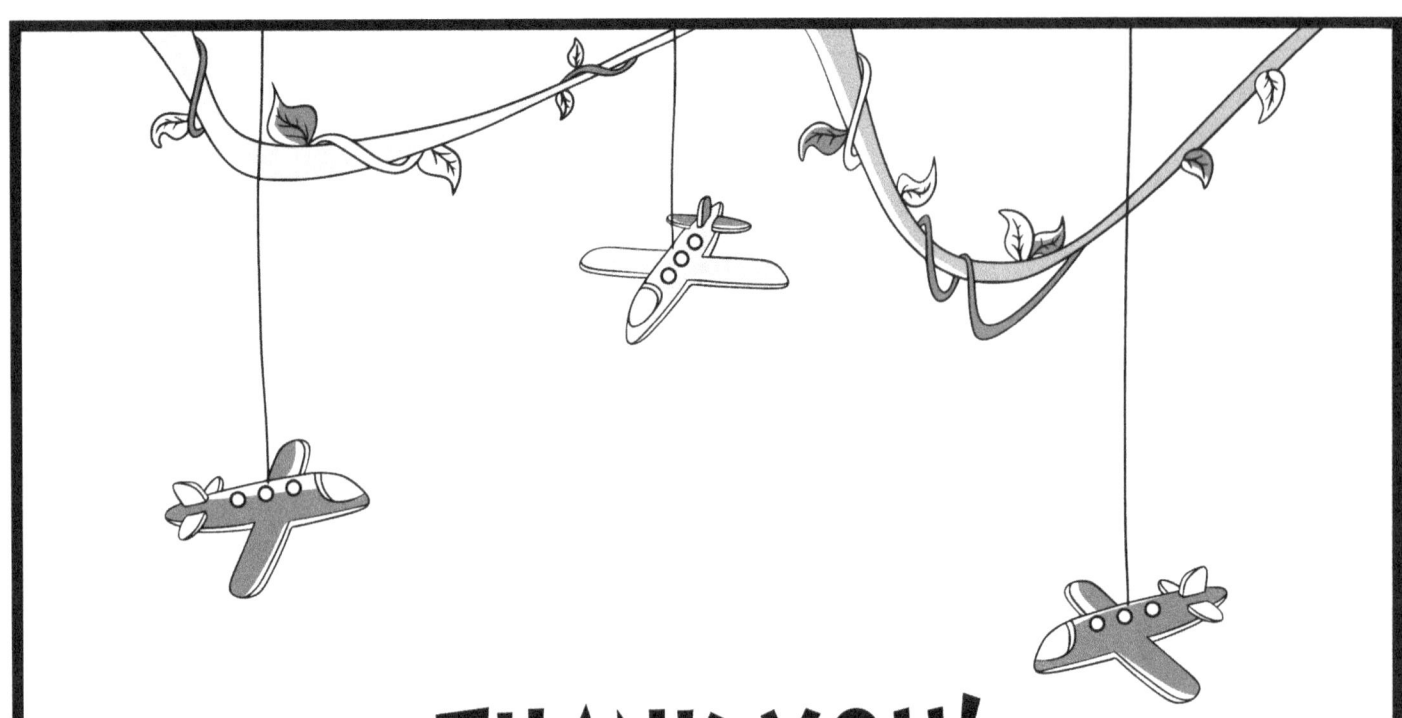

THANK YOU!

We hope you enjoyed the book.
Please consider leaving a review
where you bought it!

For more, please visit:
activitywizo.com

www.ingramcontent.com/pod-product-compliance
Lightning Source LLC
Chambersburg PA
CBHW081744100526
44592CB00015B/2297